WHY JESUS WEPT

RENO OMOKRI

REV MEDIA
PUBLISHING

WHY JESUS WEPT

RevMedia Publishing
P.O. Box 5172
Kingwood, TX 77325
www.revmediapublishing.com

ISBN: 978-0-9904764-5-0
eBook ISBN: 978-0-9904764-6-7
Printed in the United States of America
© 2015 by Reno Omokri

Mind of Christ Christian Center
PO BOX 863
Brentwood, CA 94513
www.renoomokri.org

1 2 3 4 5 6 7 8 9 10 11   21 20 19 18 17 16 15 14

"Reno is one of the most thoughtful, intelligent and well-meaning people I have met. I very much look forward to the arrival of his new book with great anticipation"-Michael Moszynski CEO and Founder, London, The Drum Awards UK Advertising Agency of the Year (2014)

"I met Reno at a divinely arranged meeting at an airport. Our love for God caused us to go into a deep conversation about God and the Kingdom. Then I read from his manuscript which became this book and I was blessed and you would too if you read it"-The Reverend Canon Precious Omuku, Adviser Anglican Communion Affairs to the Archbishop of Canterbury.

DEDICATION

This book is dedicated to my mother, Mercy, who showed me so much love and is more responsible than any other human for putting me on the narrow path that leads to life.

This book is also dedicated to my three children, Tsola, Misan and Tosan. The love for God that my mother inculcated in me has been passed on to my children and they make me so proud.

I also thank my best friend, Tuokpe, who has been God's gift to me to the end that I enjoy the abundant life.

Finally, I thank my brother Boyowa and Eta Uso Junior. A friend gifted me by the Internet who eventually became an asset to my life as a pastor and as one of the voices of a very effective President.

FOREWORD

Recently I purchased a new lap top as my old lap top was very slow and did not seem to be functioning very efficiently. I do not profess to be an expert when it comes to technology, but I assumed I could at least install the needed software without much difficulty. "This shouldn't be hard" I presumed. But when I had installed the software and attempted to open it, it would not work. I actually spent hours trying to bring it up and make it function correctly. I asked for help, but those who helped had no greater understanding of this software than I did. Finally, I went to the tried and true, I went to the bookstore and purchased a manual pertaining to the installation of the software. Maybe you relate? Possibly you would have told me, 'Why didn't you just go on line and down load the manual?' I guess I'm kind of old school, but through the manual I learned that I simply needed to change a couple of settings which were different from previous generation of that software.

It seems like manuals are a necessity if we want to be able to properly use almost any technological or mechanical item

The same is true for us humans. The Bible says that we were created by God in His image for His glory. But without proper instructions, we fail to function as God first intended. As a result, God supplied us with a manual that we might know how He intended for us to live our lives. The manual that was supplied with this model of humanity is the Bible.

In II Timothy we find three verses that give us instructions for how to use the manual. The first is II Timothy 3:16. It says that "all scripture is inspired by God..." Literally, that means that all of the Bible is God breathed. It came to us from the manufacturer, our creator. In verse 17 it provides us the purpose for our manual. It is "so the man of God may be adequate, equipped for every good work." We might change the word adequate for the word fitted, or suitable. The word adequate seems to say to me, he is okay for the good work. Fitted or suitable would seem to mean that he is truly prepared for the good work, whatever it is that God might have in mind. To be equipped would mean to furnish perfectly. In other words, God's word furnishes me with everything I will need to be suitably fitted to accomplish and become all that my creator intended me to be.

A third verse is II Timothy 2:15, which says, "Be diligent", that is make every effort, work hard, "to present yourselves approved", to present yourself fully acceptable, "to God, a workman who does not need to be ashamed." Why doesn't he need to be ashamed? Because he works hard to study and understand the Bible and apply the principles of the Word of God to his life continuously. The word to handle accurately means to cut it straight. That means we must be diligent in our study of God's Word, the Bible, to make sure that not only do we interpret it correctly but that we also apply it to our daily lives correctly.

The manual that God has given to us teaches us to live out our lives on a daily basis. There is no other manual that can do this. If we try to replace the Bible with any other manual it will lead to failure. The only manual for this model of humanity is the Bible.

As I read through "Why Jesus Wept" I was impressed with how the book was dedicated to assisting us determine Biblical principles for how we are to live Too often we read the Bible as an intellectual exercise without seeking the application which God intended for us to follow. As you read "Why Jesus Wept," I encourage you to keep a Bible and a notebook handy so that you can jot down principles that you can apply to your life and confirm them by the Word of God as you become a II Timothy 2:15 student of the word yourself.

I trust that you enjoy "Why Jesus Wept" as much as I have.

Andrew L. Cochran

Pastor, Brentwood Bible Fellowship.

CONTENTS

INTRODUCTION

Genesis 37:3-4 says, "Israel loved Joseph more than all his children, because he was the son of his old age: and he made him a coat of many colors. And when his brethren saw that their father loved him more than all his brethren, they hated him."

This verse is telling us much more than what it seems to be saying on the surface.

Joseph was hated by his brothers because he was loved by his father, and he was loved by his dad "because he was the son of his old age."

Of course, our God does not grow old, but we can see a pattern here. Mankind is loved by God above every other created being, and we were the last created beings to be made by God. We may not be the child of God's old age, but we are the children of the last day of creation.

The crux of the matter is revealed in Psalm 8:4 and 6: "What is man, that thou art mindful of him? and the son of man, that thou visitest him? ... Thou madest him to have dominion over the works of thy hands; thou hast put all things under his feet." Satan saw that God loved us more than him and gave us "dominion over the works of His hands" and "put all things under our feet.'" Therefore, he hated us. That is the genesis of Satan's hatred, the reason he seeks to ruin our lives, and keep us separate from God.

Satan hates those whom God loves. Look at the life of Yeshu'a. Satan never came to tempt Yeshu'a until after He came out of the baptismal waters of the Jordan and heard God say, "This is my beloved Son, in whom I am well pleased." This was the signal for Satan to afflict Yeshu'a, and it is the same reason Satan afflicts you and me. (In this book, I use the names Jesus and Yeshu'a interchangeably. Yeshu'a is the original Aramaic name that Jesus would have been called by His parents, His siblings, and all who knew Him. "Jesus" is derived from the Greek version of His name, Iesous.)

But how do we overcome Satan's hatred for us? The same way Joseph overcame his brothers' hatred? This question is answered in Genesis 45:3: "Joseph said to his brothers, 'I am Joseph! Is my father still living?' But his brothers were not able to answer him, because they were terrified at his presence." By fulfilling his potential and becoming so powerful in Egypt, Joseph's brothers went from hatred of him to fear of him. Joseph walked in the dominion that God had given him in Egypt.

If you learn to walk in the dominion that God has already given you, Satan will not only hate you, he will also fear you.

This is corroborated by Yeshu'a in John 10:10: "The thief cometh not, but for to steal, and to kill, and to destroy: I am come that they might have life, and that they might have it more abundantly."

But if you do not learn to walk in your God-given dominion, you will fear Satan, allowing him to steal your dominion, kill your dreams, and destroy God's purpose in your life.

Why was Joseph able to walk in dominion? The Bible is very clear: because his father loved him, which caused him to love his father in return. That created a cycle of trust between them, so that the father believed in the son, and the son believed in the father.

That is the relationship God longs to have with us. We did not begin loving God until we first experienced His love. First John 4:19 says, "We love because he first loved us."

What does love produce? John 3:16 answers that question. "For God so loved the world, that he gave his only begotten Son, that whosoever believeth in him should not perish, but have everlasting life." Love makes you have faith, and God's greatest pleasure is that we have faith in Him. The reverse is also true. God's greatest displeasure is to be doubted.

When you begin to read the first chapter of this book, you will learn the real reason why Jesus wept in the town of Bethany, and how acting on that knowledge can revolution-ize your life. It is as Jesus said in John 8:32: "You shall know the truth and the truth shall make you free!" In this book, you will learn biblical principles that will empower you to walk in your God-given dominion, beginning with the principle of belief.

Every chapter addresses a different principle, a key to the kingdom, and in detail gives practical ways that you can apply it in your everyday life. If you put these kingdom keys into practice, it is assured that the rest of your life will be the best of your life. I do not make this promise. The Son of God does. I only echo it as His ambassador because it worked in my life, and it will work in yours.

Reno Omokri

January 2015

WHY JESUS WEPT

In my experience in the ministry, the biblical incident that has been most misunderstood is the narrative of Jesus and the raising of Lazarus in Bethany. Many believers read that incident found in John chapter 11 and attribute the fact that Jesus wept at the tomb to His sadness at the death of Lazarus, His friend.

But is that the case?

If you read John 11:11, it is clear that Jesus already knew Lazarus was dead before he arrived. Furthermore, from that verse we know that Jesus had the intention to resurrect Lazarus before he left for Bethany. For this reason, He refused to go to Bethany after He received word from Mary and Martha that "the one you love is sick." In verse 6, we read that "he stayed where he was two more days" (NIV).

Jesus could have upped and left immediately to Bethany to prevent Lazarus from dying, but He had a greater purpose.

In John 11:15, Jesus lets us understand that He wanted to go to Bethany where Martha and Mary lived because He wanted them to believe.

Now, to understand why Jesus wept, we need to understand Hebrews 11:6. In this verse, the author, speaking under the anointing of the Holy Ghost, wrote, "And without faith it is impossible to please God, because anyone who comes to him must believe that he exists and that he rewards those who earnestly seek him."

From this verse, we see that God's greatest pleasure is to be believed. This personality trait is shared by His Son, Jesus.

How do I know this?

In Matthew 10:5, we read: "These twelve Jesus sent out with the following instructions: 'Do not go among the Gentiles or enter any town of the Samaritans.'" Jesus told His disciples not to enter into any Samaritan village because He wanted the gospel to be taken first to the Jews. However, in John chapter 4, Jesus encountered the Samaritan woman at the well outside of Sychar. After He had preached to her and converted her, she ran into the city and told the men there about Jesus. They came and met Him by the well and also heard Him preach. After listening to Him, verse 39 says, "Many of the Samaritans from that town believed in him because of the woman's testimony, 'He told me everything I ever did.'"

Now, in the next verses, we see something strange. Although Jesus had told His disciples not to enter into any of the Samaritan cities, we understand from these verses that after the Samaritans believed in Jesus, they invited Him into their city. Verse 40 reads: "So when the Samaritans came to him, they urged him to stay with them, and he stayed two days."

The reason Jesus agreed to enter and then stay in a Samaritan city was because the people of that city had believed in Him, which gave Him so much pleasure He was willing to go against His own admonition to His disciples.

Faith or belief pleases God and Jesus, and will compel them to "change the rules."

This brings us back to Lazarus. The reason Jesus wept is because when He got to Bethany, He was met with limited belief from Martha, Mary, and His disciples.

To put what happened in Bethany into perspective, it may be necessary to read John 20:29: "Jesus said unto him, Thomas, because you have seen me, you have believed: blessed are they that have not seen, and yet have believed."

Thomas did not trust Jesus, who is the Son of God. He wanted confirmation before he believed. But God wants us to take His words in the Bible at face value and believe without waiting for a dream, a prophet to confirm it, or some other sign. An angel or a dream is not greater than God's revealed Word.

You see, when in verse 21 Martha said, "Lord if you had been there, my brother had not died," she betrayed the fact that she had limited belief in Jesus. She felt He was limited by space and time. If she had total belief, she would have known that Jesus did not need to be physically present to stop the death of Lazarus. Martha, at that time, with all due respect, did not understand the type of faith that pleases God and His Son, Jesus.

In Matthew 8:5-10 we read: "when Jesus had entered Capernaum, a centurion came to him, asking for help. 'Lord,' he said, 'my servant lies at home paralyzed, suffering terribly.' Jesus said to him, 'Shall I come and heal him?' The centurion replied, 'Lord, I do not deserve to have you come under my roof. But just say the word, and my servant will be healed. For I myself am a man under authority, with soldiers under me. I tell this one, "Go," and he goes; and that one, "Come," and he comes. I say to my servant, "Do this," and he does it.' When Jesus heard this, he was amazed and said to those following him, 'Truly I tell you, I have not found anyone in Israel with such great faith.'"

The centurion of Matthew chapter 8.believed that Jesus was able to heal and sustain life irrespective of the limitations of space and time. This, according to Jesus, is faith that pleased Him. It is total faith, not substantial faith. This was the major difference between the sisters, Mary and Martha, and the centurion of Matthew chapter 8. Mary and Martha had substantial faith in Jesus. They believed that if He were physically present, He would have healed their brother. But the centurion believed that Jesus could heal and sustain life irrespective of any constraint.

This was the reason Jesus wept: if faith pleases Him, then doubt hurts Him. Jesus was confronted with limited faith and some doubt in Bethany, and He wept because of it—not because Lazarus was dead. He had already said days before the incident that He would resurrect his friend.

So many believers are waiting to see the physical manifestation of their prayers, hopes, and aspirations, but in too many of such cases, we are like Mary and Martha. I pray that God opens our eyes to understand the import of what Jesus said in John 11:40 to Martha.

Jesus gave a command to the grave attendants to open up Lazarus' grave. Rather than obey, Martha communicated her doubts to Jesus, telling Him in verse 39: "But, Lord, by this time there is a bad odor, for he has been there four days."

Jesus' response to Martha is so telling. He said, "Did I not tell you that if you believe, you will see the glory of God?"

Too many believers are like Martha—so focused on the natural course of events that they forget they are dealing with a supernatural God. After praying for God's intervention in our lives, many of us refuse to take the very actions that God has commanded us to take. We are looking at relationships and saying that they are long dead and forgotten when God is saying that we should revive them. We are taking our age into account and saying that it is impossible to do this or that at my age, forgetting that from age to age God is still the same.

The truth is, we can only see the glory of God if we believe. And we only believe when we obey God, irrespective of our circumstances. Remember, He wants total belief not substantial belief.

For a deeper insight into what Jesus said in John 11:40, we may want to look at 1 Corinthians 13:12 in the NIV. That verse reads: "For now we see only a reflection as in a mirror; then we shall see face to face. Now I know in part; then I shall know fully, even as I am fully known." The spiritual realm, the Word of God, which Jesus said is spirit and is life, is often compared to a mirror in the Bible. We have just read one verse of Scripture and now let us consider James 1:23-24. It says: "Anyone who listens to the word but does not do what it says is like someone who looks at his face in a mirror and, after looking at himself, goes away and immediately forgets what he looks like."

If you are familiar with mirrors, you will understand that a mirror image (a reflection) is the exact replica of what it reflects, only in reverse. So, because of the reverse reflection, if I hold a number plate that reads 321, it will reflect back in the mirror as 123.

The mirror figuratively represents the spiritual realm, as we see in 1 Corinthians 13:12 and James 1:23-24. Just like the mirror, the spiritual gives you a reflection of the physical realm. However, the physical realm cannot reflect the mirror because the spiritual governs the physical. That is why the mirror reflects the physical (but remember that the reflection is in reverse).

In the natural, you see to believe, but in the spiritual that is reflected back to you when you look at the perfect law of liberty, which is the Word of God, the reverse is true. You believe to see.

In the natural, you have to climb your way to the top, but in the spiritual, you humble yourself by going down. Then God takes you up by exalting you.

In the natural, you take from people to get rich, but in the spiritual, you give to people to become wealthy.

In the natural, you are reactive, but in the spiritual, you are proactive.

The reason for this fundamental difference between a natural man and a spiritual man is that spiritual things are spiritually discerned, but to the natural man they are foolishness.

Do you remember what Jesus told Nicodemus in John 3:12? He said, "I have spoken to you of earthly things and you do not believe; how then will you believe if I speak of heavenly things?"

Jesus, wept because of doubt, and while I do not think it is possible to weep in heaven, I know from Scripture that the only time a witness describes what appears to be a party in heaven is when a sinner repents and becomes a believer (see Luke 15:70). Belief is central to God.

Adam and Eve fell from grace because they did not believe God, preferring instead to believe the serpent. Abraham believed God, and it was accounted unto him for righteousness.

Even with us as humans, we do not like it when people do not believe in us. This is because we are made in the image of God. It saddens us when people doubt us, particularly in areas where we know we have capacity. And it saddens God when we doubt Him in any way at all, because while we have limited capacity, God has unlimited capacity and can do all things.

Never doubt God!

SOW MONEY AND BE RICH; SOW TIME AND BE WEALTHY

Being conscious of your time on Earth focuses your mind and helps you to put things into perspective in a way that facilitates wisdom. In Psalm 90:12, we read: "Teach us to number our days, that we may gain a heart of wisdom." But how many of us really number our days? How many of us are conscious of the times that we live in?

When we do not number our days, they creep up on us and feed patterns of worry. And worry is a sin. God does not want us to worry about tomorrow. He wants us to plan for tomorrow, and the best way to do so is to be conscious of time, because time was created for this material realm.

God not only wants us to number our days, He also wants us to monitor the resources He has blessed us with as faithful stewards. In Proverbs 27:23, we read the admonition: "Be sure you know the condition of your flocks, give careful attention to your herds."

To understand the thrust of this chapter, let me first state that nobody owns anything on earth. We are just stewards as we read in Psalm 24:1: "The earth is the LORD's, and every-thing in it, the world, and all who live in it."

So now, we see that God wants us to number our days and pay attention to the state of our material possessions. But why?

Did you have the experience in school when you were supposed to be reading and studying every day, but you did not do that? So when examinations were just around the corner you started to cram, and you ended up passing the examinations. I did. Most people, if they are honest did too. The trouble with that learning method is that you get a diploma, but you did not gain the intrinsic benefits of your education. Or, in other words, you didn't learn anything.

It is the same when we do not number our days. We grow old, but we do not grow wise.

Therefore, if we are not conscious of what we are doing with our days, hours, minutes and seconds, we are not numbering our days.

The greater sin with God is to waste time, not money, because you can always make more money. But you cannot make more time.

Money has so blinded our society that people prefer to number (count) their money rather than their time. As soon as they acquire money, most people, who think they are wise, begin to make a budget. To most people, a budget is just a plan to use money prudently. But what about a time budget—a plan to prudently use time?

I have studied the habits of wealthy people. There is a difference between a wealthy person and a rich person. Wealthy people control the assets that produce money, while rich people just have money.

Tomorrow, any currency can be devalued, and the holder of money becomes poor. Assets, however, hold their value even when money is devalued, because the worth of assets are recalculated to reflect the new value of money. That's why the wealthy hardly ever lose their wealth, but rich people frequently lose their riches.

So, what did I learn from studying the wealthy?

The basic difference between the wealthy and the rich is that the wealthy budget their time, while the rich budget their money. Since time is more valuable than money, the wealthy are devoting the best part of their intellectual and spiritual intelligence in managing what is more precious, and this ensures that they have a constant supply of everything that time influences.

The rich, on the other hand, spend the best part of their intellectual and spiritual resources managing money, and are, therefore, at the mercy of time, which is spiritually more dominant and materially more precious than money.

Ecclesiastes 3:1 teaches us that there is a time for everything: "To everything there is a season, and a time to every purpose under the heaven." This verse is really saying more than we think it is saying. While there is a time for everything, there isn't money for everything. So value time over money, and you will have influence over things.

Have you ever heard of the job title, Money Manager? A money manager is someone who manages other people's money and places them on a budget. I learned that wealthy people usually have a money manager. You know what that does for the wealthy? It frees up their minds so that they can manage their time.

In 2013, for the first time ever, and then again in 2014, Apple overtook ExxonMobil as the world's most valuable company. Steve Jobs was a man who changed the world through the inventions and products of Apple. He was also one of the world's richest men. Listen to what he had to say about time and money: "My favorite things in life do not cost any money. It's really clear that the most precious resource we all have is time."

I propose that more than all the anointing that some in the Pentecostal realm engage in in the name of the prosperity gospel, you are more likely to have the John 10:10 abundant life if you sow your time properly. You reap what you sow. If you sow money, you will reap money and everything that is under money. If you sow time, you will reap time and everything that is under time, including money.

Let me use myself as an example.

I used to have a regular nine-to-five job. In fact, mine was eight to whenever I finished my work. I was earning overtime. I would leave my house very early at 5:30 a.m. on the dot so I could beat rush hour traffic and arrive at work on time. I would stay late, because if I left at four in the afternoon, I would be stuck in San Francisco rush hour traffic. This continued for four years. And then, I began to practice what I was reading in the Bible.

In Genesis 8:22, I read that "as long as the earth endures, seedtime and harvest, cold and heat, summer and winter, day and night will never cease."

I took quite literally, what the Bible says in Hebrews 12:2 and looked unto Jesus, studying the way He spent His life. More than anything else, other than His sacrificial death, Jesus served God with His time. He would commune with God alone and at length every morning and every evening. He would honor every God-ordained time for assembly of the brethren. He took time to meditate, even when asked questions by His disciples and skeptics.

I realized from reading the Gospels that while many in Christendom now focus on sowing money, they will never find one instance where Jesus sowed money. In John 13:39, we read that Jesus had a money manager. "Since Judas had charge of the money, some thought Jesus was telling him to buy what was needed for the festival, or to give something to the poor." Jesus personally sowed time to God, and as He did that, God provided Judas Iscariot, whose job it was to sow money on His behalf.

Does this not remind you of how the wealthy of today behave? From whom do you think they learned this principle? Of course, they learned it from the Son of God!

So, I started to devote more and more time to God. I devoted not the leftovers of my time, but, as much as I could, I devoted the premium hours of my time.

And then, after four years of time-consuming work, God gave me a break. I got a client who allowed me to work from home, and after I worked on this client's election, he won and offered me a job that affords me enough time to devote to God. Because I have time to devote to God, I am able today to have someone who helps me manage my money while I manage my time.

You see the principle? Sow money and be rich, sow time and be wealthy.

Ephesians 5:16 encourages believers to "redeem the time, because the days are evil." We are asked to make the best use of time. What is the best use of time? What can be better than using it to serve God?

People who understand the value of time use it well in serving God and, like Paul, they can say at their life's end what Paul said in 2 Timothy 4:7: "I have fought the good fight, I have finished the race, I have kept the faith." You do not want to get to the end of your life and only then realize that the money you thought had value was, in fact, just ordinary paper. Think back to the very last words of Bob Marley, spoken to Ziggy, his son. He said, "Money can't buy life." This is the true story of the last seconds of Bob Marley's life. It should not be the true story of your life. You should realize that before you lie on your deathbed.

In Luke 12:16-20, Jesus delivered the parable of the rich fool. "And he told them this parable: 'The ground of a certain rich man yielded an abundant harvest. He thought to himself, "What shall I do? I have no place to store my crops." Then he said, "This is what I'll do. I will tear down my barns and build bigger ones, and there I will store my surplus grain. And I'll say to myself, 'You have plenty of grain laid up for many years. Take life easy; eat, drink and be merry.'" But God said to him, 'You fool! This very night your life will be demanded from you. Then who will get what you have prepared for yourself?'"

What is life? Life is the time you spend in this material realm before you enter the realm of eternal life. There is a difference between life and eternal life. Life on earth is just that—life. Life in God's kingdom is eternal life.

In essence, what Bob Marley was saying to his son, Ziggy, is that money cannot buy the time you spend in this material realm. However, the time you spend in this material realm can both buy money and eternal life if the time is well invested.

So, the question now is how do we best invest our time so that it gives us the best returns here and in the life to come?

Just as God expects His children to tithe the very first part of their income to Him as an act of worship, God wants us to tithe the very first minutes of our day to Him. This is the fuller meaning of Matthew 6:33, which says: "But seek first his kingdom and his righteousness, and all these things will be given to you as well."

So, when you wake up each day, before you do anything that matters only in this realm, set aside time for God. From your bed, go to your knees. From your knees go to your Bible, and only then should you have time to devote to earthly matters.

Repeat the same process every night.

Also, we have to practice the customs of Jesus. The Bible clearly tells us about Jesus' customs during His earthly life. Let us examine them and compare them to our own customs.

In Luke 4:16 we read: "He went to Nazareth, where he had been brought up, and on the Sabbath day he went into the synagogue, as was his custom." From this, we read that it was Jesus' custom to always be at the synagogue during the regular assembly. Can that be said about us? Do we have that custom? Or are we one of those who are mostly in church, sometimes in church, but not always in church? Was that the example that Jesus gave us?

Let us look at another of His customs. In Luke 22:39 we read: "Jesus went out as usual to the Mount of Olives." We see that it was Jesus' custom to regularly go to the mountaintop for a retreat with His Father. Do you ever take time out to retreat yourself from the world so that you can advance toward God?

Jesus' apostles also copied His lifestyle. In Acts 17:2, we read: "As was his custom, Paul went into the synagogue, and on three Sabbath days he reasoned with them from the Scriptures."

But above all else, Jesus spent His life winning souls for God.

Have you ever spent time doing that? If you can share your gossip with others, what defense will you have before God when He asks you why you did not share the Gospel with others?

What other thing did Jesus spend His time doing? Jesus constantly praised God. As a matter of fact, whenever Jesus performed a miracle, the people around would praise God in fulfillment of Matthew 5:16: "In the same way, let your light shine before others, that they may see your good deeds and glorify your Father in heaven."

Still on the issue of praise, did you know that one of the reasons God made man is to receive praise from us?

Let us examine it. In Genesis 1:4 we read: "God saw that the light was good." In Genesis 1:31 we also read: "God saw all that he had made, and it was very good." Do you know what God was doing? He was praising Himself. God praised Himself when He had not yet made man. After making man, the responsibility and joy of praising God shifted from God to man.

Notice what God said after He created creation. He said "it is good" and "it is very good." Now, notice what Jesus says in Mark 10:18. He said, "Why do you call me good? No one is good—except God alone." Good—the same word God used to describe Himself and His creation when He began creating creation. What Jesus is teaching us in that verse is the habit of giving glory and praise to God. Do you spend your time seeking your own glory or God's glory?

God loves praise, but He does not like flattery, and when people who haven't spent time to study His attributes praise Him, they are actually flattering Him, and He does not delight or dwell in that form of praise.

Let us read Psalm 150 for inspiration on how to praise God.

Praise the Lord.

Praise God in his sanctuary;

praise him in his mighty heavens.

Praise him for his acts of power;

praise him for his surpassing greatness.

Praise him with the sounding of the trumpet,

praise him with the harp and lyre,

praise him with timbrel and dancing,

praise him with the strings and pipe,

praise him with the clash of cymbals,

praise him with resounding cymbals.

Let everything that has breath praise the Lord.

Praise the Lord.

Notice that in this psalm David is very specific. He details why he praises God. He is not ambiguous. He proves that he has studied God's nature. He is intimate with God. Every praise that is not from intimacy is shallow.

Perhaps there is nothing wrong in seeking your own glory, but it must be done under the banner of seeking God's glory. Therefore, if you delight yourself in the things that you are doing for God, He has promised to give you the desires of your heart (see Psalm 37:4).

EVOLVING FROM SERVANTHOOD TO FRIENDSHIP WITH GOD

In John 7:48-49, we read why the Pharisees refused to accept Jesus as the Messiah. They said to the soldiers (who had been sent to arrest Him but returned believing in Him) thus: "Have any of the rulers or of the Pharisees believed in him? No! But this mob that knows nothing of the law—there is a curse on them."

From this verse, we understand that what was causing the Pharisees and the rulers not to believe was their knowledge of the law. You see, holding on to the law causes unbelief.

Let us go deeper. In Genesis 15:6, we read, "Abram believed the LORD, and he credited it to him as righteousness." From this Scripture, we see that it was an act of faith, or belief, that caused God to credit Abraham with righteousness. Why? Because God's greatest pleasure is to be believed. Abraham existed before the law. He did not live under the law. The law came by Moses.

Do you know why God introduced the law? Exodus 15:24 tells us the reason in part: "So the people grumbled against Moses, saying, 'What are we to drink?'" Exodus 16:2 continues the reason: "In the desert the whole community grumbled against Moses and Aaron." Finally, Exodus 32:9-10 finishes the reason: "I have seen these people," the LORD said to Moses, "and they are a stiff-necked people. Now leave me alone so that my anger may burn against them and that I may destroy them. Then I will make you into a great nation."

The ancient Israelites were the heirs of the promise that God made to Abraham and his descendants. However, they were a very rebellious and difficult people. They constantly sinned against God, and it came to a point that God came close to wiping them out. So, to protect them from His anger, it was necessary for God to give them ground rules. Thus, the law was introduced.

Even in the law, God introduced elements of grace that projected his loving nature. It was not His intention that the harshness of the law would be everlasting.

In read Hebrews 11:39 we read: "These were all commended for their faith, yet none of them received what had been promised." From this, we see that approval always comes through faith, and since those who are invested in the law have a hard time having faith, our investments should rather be in grace through faith.

We all may have to consider that Satan knows the law, but he does not know grace. So when we are legalistic and facetious when people break the law, consider that we are not at that particular time operating from grace. We are operating from law, and that spirit is not from God.

Pardon people. Be gracious to them.

Although we might think that the law was some great thing, we need to understand that grace through faith is an even better thing, and the Bible proves this. Throughout the Old Testament, there were two people who stood out as the epitome of grace (even though Christ had not yet come).

The first was Abraham, who believed God, and it was accounted unto him as righteousness. The second was David, who had a special relationship with God, because among other things, he ignored the law and loved God. He ate the shew bread that the law said was not legal for him to eat. He was a man who told of his ability to enter into God's gate with thanksgiving and His court with praise, not because of his obedience to the Law.

Now compare these three men, Abraham, David, and Moses. Abraham was a man under grace, and look at what God called him in Isaiah 41:8: "But you, Israel, my servant, Jacob, whom I have chosen, you descendants of Abraham my friend." He called Abraham His friend. David was a man under grace and look at what God called him in 1 Samuel 13:14: "The LORD has sought out a man after his own heart and appointed him ruler of his people." He called him a man after His own heart.

Now Moses was also under the law, but look what God called him in Deuteronomy 34:5: "Moses the servant of the LORD." God called Moses "a servant of God."

Look at the difference. Friend, man after His heart, and then, servant.

To know the implication of this, look at what Jesus said in John 15:15: "I no longer call you servants, I call you friends instead." Jesus is saying in that verse that when you come to know Him, you move from the law to grace, and you get promoted from being a servant, a slave to the law, very legalistic, to being a partaker of grace with all the freedoms that it brings. Then, like Paul, you can say: "There is therefore now no condemnation to them which are in Christ Jesus, who walk not after the flesh, but after the Spirit" (Romans 8:1).

The flesh is the law and the Spirit is grace, hence, 2 Corinthians 3:6 says, "the letter killeth, but the spirit giveth life."

On the surface, you might not get the implication of these distinctions. But let us read Joshua 4:14: "On that day the LORD magnified Joshua in the sight of all Israel; and they feared him, as they feared Moses, all the days of his life" (KJV). Now let us consider John 21:7: "Then the disciple whom Jesus loved said to Peter, 'It is the Lord!'" In John 21:15 we also read the following exchange: "Jesus said to Simon Peter, 'Simon son of John, do you love me more than these?' 'Yes, Lord,' he said, 'you know that I love you.' Jesus said, 'Feed my lambs.'" Notice that the people feared Moses, but Jesus loved His people and He also wanted them to love Him.

God created us for fellowship, and fellowship must lead to friendship; otherwise, it is not fellowship. We must grow in our relationship with God in a continuum of maturity. The truth is, when we have not served God with diligence, we cannot grow from being a servant to being a friend. It is a process. You are promoted from one level to another.

Notice the relationship of absolute trust that existed between God and Abraham and God and David. They didn't start out being God's friends. They grew into being His friends.

But the issue with a lot of humanity, and even Christians, and maybe especially church-going persons, is that we would rather be masters over other people rather than master ourselves enough to serve God diligently.

Part of being a good servant, a good steward of God, is how you superintend those whom God has placed you over in a position of authority. When you have authority over a person or people, you need to do more to bridle your tongue, because whether we know it or not, there is power in the tongue.

As a parent, husband, pastor, boss, or leader, we must make every effort to obey God's admonition to "bless and do not curse" (Romans 12:14). You might think your words are just idle, but remember that Jesus said, "Every idle word that men shall speak, they shall give account thereof in the day of judgment" (Matthew 12:36). Why did Jesus say so? Because He knows that there is no such thing as an idle word.

If you want to know how much power your words possess, then read this exchange between God and our first human parent: "Now the LORD God had formed out of the ground all the wild animals and all the birds in the sky. He brought them to the man to see what he would name them; and whatever the man called each living creature, that was its name"(Genesis 2:19). When your children, wife, employees or congregants begin to display tendencies or behaviors similar to the words that you have used on them, do not immediately blame them. Examine your past words over them. Perhaps their current behavior is a consequence of your past words. However, because there is a process of time involved before your words manifest in reality, you may not recognize the connection. To change their behavior for the better, do not just shout, criticize and intimidate your subordinates. Instead, change your words over them from negative to positive.

Do not boast about how much of the letter of the Word of God you know. Instead, boast about how much of God's grace you have experienced. That is the hidden meaning behind Jeremiah 9:24: "But let the one who boasts boast about this: that they have the understanding to know me, that I am the LORD, who exercises kindness, justice and righteousness on earth, for in these I delight, declares the LORD."

So, notice again what happened in John 7:48-49. The chief priests sent soldiers to take Jesus, but when these soldiers got to Jesus, they were in awe of what He taught and said. They refused to arrest Him! When they returned, the chief priests were mad at them and said that they shouldn't have believed in Jesus since the rulers had not believed in Him.

Acts 10:34 says: "Then Peter opened his mouth, and said, 'Of a truth I perceive that God is no respecter of persons.'" God is no respecter of persons. That a person is a man of influence in this world does not mean he has greater access to God than you do. You and I have equal and unlimited access to God's Word. And when you read the Bible and it appears so simple to you, do not be intimidated by the simplicity you see in the Word and think that it is only appearing simple to you because you are of a simple nature and are not very sophisticated. No. It is simple to you because the Word of God is simple and easy to be understood. The problem with most people is that they mistrust simple things and take it to men who will bamboozle them with their knowledge of the law, making complicated what was designed to be simple and stripping it of the power inherent in it.

Second Corinthians 11:3 says: "I fear, lest by any means, as the serpent beguiled Eve through his subtlety, so your minds should be corrupted from the simplicity that is in Christ." Once a doctrine, a prophecy, or some other ecclesiastical matter starts being complicated, that is an indication God is raising a red flag. All ecclesiastical matters are designed by God to be simple. They are simple to understand but require discipline to undertake.

On the other hand, things of the Enemy are complicated, yet they require no discipline.

So when you read Scripture, take it at face value. If God says something, and His Spirit ministers to you that this is for you, do not hesitate because you are not a pastor or a great evangelist. Trust that the Holy Spirit is guiding you.

Psalm 8:2 says: "Through the praise of children and infants you have established a stronghold against your enemies, to silence the foe and the avenger." Jesus Himself referred to this Scripture in Matthew 21:16: "'Do you hear what these children are saying?' they asked him. 'Yes,' replied Jesus, 'have you never read, "From the lips of children and infants you, Lord, have called forth your praise?"'"

Many have allowed manipulative people to twist Scripture in order to control them and influence their choices of a marriage partner, business decisions, and other such sundry decisions that God has equipped us with enough grace to handle ourselves. We meet with such people for counseling because, for example, we find a life partner. Because they have a corporate agenda to ensure that tithes, collections, and offerings never reduce, they have formed a habit of frowning on any marriage outside their local church. So, they will ask you, "Are you sure that you heard from God before choosing so and so as your life partner?"

Or, you go and meet them to discuss something that God has placed in your heart to do. And although you went to them with certainty, you return full of doubts. Can you imagine that God has given you an instruction, and you know that you heard from God, yet you allow a man to turn you away from what God has told you! Why?

Or, imagine that Scripture has given you discretion on a particular matter and, rather than exercise the discretion that Scripture has given you, you now fall under the dominion of a man.

Second Peter 2:14 warns us of such people as "having eyes full of adultery, and that cannot cease from sin; beguiling unstable souls: an heart they have exercised with covetous practices; cursed children" (KJV).

Remember that old gospel song that says: trust and obey, for there's no other way to be happy in Jesus but to trust and obey. You are to trust and obey only God through Jesus. For every other person, the instruction is trust, verify and then obey, only after verification. "Now the Berean Jews were of more noble character than those in Thessalonica, for they received the message with great eagerness and examined the Scriptures every day to see if what Paul said was true" (Acts 17:11).

Prayerfully take time before making the decision as to what church to attend if you want to grow from being a servant to a friend of God. Many churches are not really churches. Some of them are cults. It does not mean that they perform occult rites or magic. No. In many cases, these churches are built around the personality of their founders and not Christ. You will discern this when you notice a great deal of time and devotion being dedicated to such persons (like a personality cult). If the church is giving glory to God through Jesus, it will be obvious because no one will share the stage with Him.

What we ought to understand is that we only have one Shepherd as Psalm 23:1 teaches us. Jesus is our only Shepherd. The instruction that we receive from the New Testament is to follow people only to the extent that they follow Christ. "Follow my example, as I follow the example of Christ" (1 Corinthians 11:1).

There is no new revelation or testament other than the New Testament. So anything anybody presents to you in the form of a doctrine of a church, or a man of God, that does not have an unobscured and firm foundation in Scripture is worthless and should be discarded. "Above all, you must understand that no prophecy of Scripture came about by the prophet's own interpretation of things" (2 Peter 1:20).

We need to understand the foundation of our faith. Second Timothy 3:16 tells us that all we need to make our faith secure is in the Bible. The reason that we know this particular Scripture is true is because there are various writers of the Bible, but they all agree with each other. This can only be possible because they had the same source of inspiration, the Holy Spirit.

Most other sacred books have just one author, so it is not possible to corroborate agreement with other similarly inspired authors.

If you search Scripture, you will never see any place where Jesus or the disciples told people who they will marry or where they would work, which career they should follow or other such matters. These are issues God will judge us on, so He has given us personal responsibilities over them. At the very most, Ephesians 1:17 makes us understand that God may intervene by revelation via His Holy Spirit. This revelation will, according to Scripture, be confirmed and will bring you inner peace rather than anxiety and worry. You will just "know." You will grow into an awareness in your spirit that this is where you ought to go.

God spoke to Cornelius that He would send Peter to him, and God confirmed it to Peter (Acts 10:4-5 and 19-20). God spoke to Ananias to go and open the eyes of Paul after he had been blinded on his way to Damascus, and God warned Paul to expect him (Acts 9:10-12). God does not reveal you as a husband or wife, business partner, or employee to somebody else without also confirming the information to you through a source independent of the person making the claim. Unfortunately, many, many, people have fallen victim to "God told me" presumptuousness and have forgotten that "In the mouth of two or three witnesses shall every word be established" (2 Corinthians 13:1).

So, we should learn discernment from these experiences recorded in the Bible so we are not tossed to and fro by people who are giving us their opinions and selling it to us as those of the Spirit. This is a hallmark of friendship with God. This is a hallmark of spiritual maturity.

If we do not know where we stand in Christ, we will be tossed to and fro by every wind of doctrine. And when Ephesians 4:14 talks about every wind of doctrine, understand that it is talking about spirits. The Bible uses wind to refer to spirits. Jesus also did the same in John 3:8. So be careful so that you are not tossed to and fro by every type of spirit.

You may say to yourself, spirits will never toss me. If you say that, you have not watched a good movie. I watched a movie recently, and I became so invested in this movie that I was rooting for one of the characters. I disliked the villain. I wanted him to get his comeuppance so badly I was leaning at the edge of my seat. I thought good thoughts for the hero character, I identified with him and his family and his trials.

But you know what? It was all make believe. The whole plot that so moved my emotions, my mind, and my body was a fable acted out by actors under the guidance of a director.

Hollywood actors and directors with their special effects are amateurs when compared to the devil and his demons.

Listen people, when we are facing drama in our life that is making us hate some people and dislike others, or align with a person or group so that we can fight our enemies or defend ourselves, what is happening is that demons are acting out a script of their director, Satan.

In order that we are not tossed to and fro by demons and their overlords, we need to resist the urge to act on emotions and sentiments, and focus on principles. Because emotions are in a state of flux, they are unstable, ever changing, and therefore, unreliable.

Focus on what never changes. Focus on God's principles. "Those who trust in the LORD are like Mount Zion, which cannot be shaken but endures forever" (Psalm 125:1).

From the book of Revelation, we understand that there is going to be a judgment of all of humanity on the day of the great white throne judgment. "And the sea gave up the dead which were in it; and death and hell delivered up the dead which were in them: and they were judged every man according to their works" (Revelations 20:13). This may seem far-fetched to some, but consider that Romans 14:12 says, "So then every one of us shall give account of himself to God."

I once worked in a firm that was audited, and we had accounts in various banks. During the process, all of our accounts were called up and audited by the external auditor. This is just a physical manifestation of what Christ will do to humanity on that day. The grave is just an account where dead souls go. You could call them accounts that have been retired. The living represent accounts where debts that have not yet been paid reside. You could call that an account receivable. On that day of judgment, Jesus (our auditor) shall call on all these accounts to be audited. And just like in an earthly audit, only those transactions that are transparent will be marked "paid in full" and approved by the auditor. Are you paid in full? Remember the words of Jesus in John 14:6: "I am the way, the truth, and the life: no man cometh unto the Father, but by me."

Jesus is not just inviting us to obtain salvation. That is only the beginning of the journey. He is saying to us, "Come as you are, but do not stay as you are. I accept you as servants, but in reality, I want you to grow to become my friends."

JUDGE YOURSELF AND LET GOD JUDGE OTHERS

Let me start out this chapter by saying a criticism spared on earth is a judgment saved in heaven. Jesus told us this much by saying, "Do not judge or you too will be judged" (Matthew 7:1 NIV).

One thing that all people, but most notably Christians, should avoid is the urge to criticize. The word itself, criticism, is just a fancy word used by the world to hide what is really being done—judging.

To criticize a thing, person or group is to judge them. You see, in law, when judges want to pass a judgment, the judgment is called an opinion. The reason why the judge's opinion becomes a judgment is that he has been appointed to judge.

That is why when Moses tried to give his opinion to the two Hebrews who were fighting, the one in the wrong asked him, "Who made you a judge over us?" (Exodus 2:14).

To render an opinion is to render a judgment. And you need to be careful about judging or criticizing others, because when you have negatively passed a judgment on them, you are judging yourself and putting yourself outside the banner of mercy.

This is what Jesus meant when He said, "Do not judge or you too will be judged" (Matthew 7:1 NIV).

You see, there is limited time to engage in self-development. We do not have any extra time. So every moment spent in criticizing others is borrowed from time and energy that should have been devoted to self-development. This is what Jesus meant when He asked us to remove the log in our own eye so we will see more clearly to remove the speck in our brother's eye. What we know about ourselves that needs changing and improvement is always more than what we see in others. Why? Because the way the world is structured is such that we look at others with magnifying glasses and on ourselves with rose-colored glasses.

Let us consider the exchange between King David and Prophet Nathan in 2 Samuel 12:1-7:

The Lord sent Nathan to David. When he came to him, he said, "There were two men in a certain town, one rich and the other poor. The rich man had a very large number of sheep and cattle, but the poor man had nothing except one little ewe lamb he had bought. He raised it, and it grew up with him and his children. It shared his food, drank from his cup and even slept in his arms. It was like a daughter to him. "Now a traveler came to the rich man, but the rich man refrained from taking one of his own sheep or cattle to prepare a meal for the traveler who had come to him. Instead, he took the ewe lamb that belonged to the poor man and prepared it for the one who had come to him." David burned with anger against the man and said to Nathan, "As surely as the Lord lives, the man who did this must die! 6He must pay for that lamb four times over, because he did such a thing and had no pity." Then Nathan said to David, "You are the man!"

Notice here that Nathan described a metaphoric situation that was actually a representation of David's personal scenario, and when David judged the matter, the prophet told him that he had judged himself.

God still uses the same mode of operation today. Many of the situations we pass judgments upon are metaphors for our own situations. If the Bible tells us that we may entertain angels unawares, is it such a great leap to imagine that we will encounter our own scenarios in others for the purpose of seeing whether we will criticize or empathize?

Everything in this world is just a matter of degrees. People are rich or poor according to degrees. People are good or evil according to degrees. Now, it is only in this world that degree matters.

For instance, do we think if a man steals a dollar, while another steals one million dollars, that one is less guilty in the eye of God than the other is? No, it is only in human eyes that it matters, not in God's eyes.

So, bearing this mind, consider the case of a man who has clothes that he is not wearing in his closet. And consider that such a man is criticizing another man for buying a private jet when he could have used the money to look after the poor around him.

Now, what is the difference between these two men? Is it not a matter of degree? You have clothes in your closet that you have not worn for a year and are not likely to wear any time in the future, yet you are criticizing the man who bought a private jet.

The devil's trick is to blind our eyes to these degrees and make us think that it matters to God.

We should never think to ourselves that we would do better than someone else would if we were in their shoes, because their full situation is not obvious to us. We only see what we see. There are things we do not see or know.

Can you imagine that you are writing an examination and, instead of facing your questions, you are looking at another person's questions and wanting to dot his i's and cross his t's? How foolish would that be?

In James 1:12, we read that life is really a test. "Blessed is the one who perseveres under trial because, having stood the test, that person will receive the crown of life that the Lord has promised to those who love him." Fellow human beings are writing their own test. It makes sense for us to focus on our own test papers and leave others to focus on theirs.

In Romans 14:4, we read: "Who are you to judge someone else's servant? To their own master, servants stand or fall. And they will stand, for the Lord is able to make them stand." Notice that the verse says, "For the Lord is able to make them stand." How many of you know that from kindergarten to college schools offer what are called re-sit exams, or remedials, or carryovers. Examiners do not want students to fail. They want them to pass, so they provide many opportunities for them to pass where they had previously failed.

In fact, in America we have a law called No Child Left Behind, which ensures that every child has a shot at passing through school, no matter their educational challenge. God has His own No Child Left Behind policy, which is what we read in Romans 14:4.

We need to understand that when we criticize we are not projecting love, which is the cardinal stone of our faith, being that God Himself is Light and His light manifests via His love.

Take John 3:16, which says: "For God so loved the world that He gave His only Son." Do you see that this means that while we were still sinners and under the judgment, God loved us enough to sacrifice Jesus for our salvation? When we judge others, we are not portraying that love. If God spared us judgment, we ought to spare others too. To refuse to do that is to be religious and claim to have faith. Contrary to popular belief, religion and faith are two different areas.

When I was a child, my siblings and I used to play a game called "do as I say, do not do as I do." In that game, you say something and do something contrary. It might have been a game, but in reality, I have seen life imitating that game. Religion is the outward appearance; faith goes to the state of the heart. It is possible to pretend to be religious, but you can't fake faith. Jesus was full of faith while the Pharisees were full of religion. Faith acts what it believes. Religion believes what it does not act. And when you constantly criticize people, you are claiming to believe in Christ but are not practicing what He said in Matthew 7:1: "Do not judge, or you too will be judged."

What some call destiny is simply God knowing in advance what will happen to us. He knows in advance, yet doesn't interfere with our choices.

So do not say that I was destined to do this and I was destined to do that. The only thing we are destined to do on earth is to be born and to face tests and trials and, if Jesus tarries, to die. All other things are a result of our choices. Once we understand this, we take full responsibility for our past and for the task of making better choices for our future, because the present is pregnant with the future.

The Devil also knows that the present is pregnant with the future. So he has plans to terminate that pregnancy by presenting us with scenarios that are allegories for our own real-life situations. He baits us to criticize those situations, whether they are in higher or lower degrees than ours. Once we swallow the bait, he uses our own words to accuse us to God as someone unworthy of the pregnancy we are carrying. This is one reason we have people pregnant with tomorrow, but that tomorrow never comes. Why? Because they have used their mouths to disqualify themselves.

And do not think that we cannot control our urge to criticize. We can. God is no respecter of persons, but humans are. We respect people. Have you ever heard someone say or perhaps you have said it yourself: "I won't take that from you!" What you are actually saying, though the meaning may be lost to your conscious mind, is that you can "take that" from some other persons, but not from that particular person. Why? Because human beings are respecters of persons.

Why not change today. Instead of being a respecter of persons, try to be like your Creator and do not be a respecter of persons. Acts 10:34 says: "Then Peter opened his mouth, and said, Of a truth I perceive that God is no respecter of persons" (KJV). Treat everyone with the same courtesy as recommended by 1 Peter 2:17: "Honor all men. Love the brotherhood. Fear God. Honor the king" (KJV).

Learn to differentiate people from what they do. You can hate what they do. Even God hates what we sometimes do. But never hate the person. If we must criticize at all, criticize what people do, never the people themselves. Conversely, praise people directly; do not just praise what they do.

Consider Jesus. The Bible records little about His earthly ministry until after His baptism by John the Baptist. As soon as Jesus came out of the water, His Father spoke from heaven saying, "This is my beloved Son, in whom I am well pleased" (Matthew 3:17). From that moment, the Bible records that "Jesus went about all Galilee, teaching in their synagogues, and preaching the gospel of the kingdom, and healing all manner of sickness and all manner of disease among the people" (Matthew 4:23). When you praise and affirm people, you empower them to do things that explode their sphere of influence and increase their productivity. Whether as a parent, a boss, or a pastor, the most sensible thing you can do to increase the effectiveness of people around you is to affirm them.

And it is so important to understand this principle, because much of the time when we are praying, our prayers are not ascending to heaven because of the critical nature of our tongue, which reveals a heart that is unforgiving and judgmental. The first criteria for forgiveness of sin is that we forgive others.

In 2 Chronicles 7:14, we see that God has ordained a principle for interaction between Him and man: "If my people, who are called by my name, will humble themselves and pray and seek my face and turn from their wicked ways, then I will hear from heaven, and I will forgive their sin and will heal their land."

God hears us only when we humble ourselves and seeks Him, which is a fulfillment of James 4:8. After hearing, He forgives us if we have forgiven others. And when He has forgiven, He moves on to heal.

Daniel also corroborates this modus operandi that God operates on in Daniel 9:19: "Lord, listen! Lord, forgive! Lord, hear and act! For your sake, my God, do not delay, because your city and your people bear your Name."

So, if we persist in being people of a critical nature, chances are that we will never get past the hear state. So, leave off criticism, not for the other person's sake, but for your own sake.

So that you can progress to forgiving and then to the healing state that God Himself talked about in 2 Chronicles 7:14 and that Daniel reiterates in Daniel 9:19.

FROM SELF-MANAGEMENT TO RELATIONSHIP MANAGEMENT

Intelligence is God's gift to you and your character is your gift to Him. Character must be differentiated from reputation. Character is what you really are, while reputation is what people think about you.

Character is more important to God than reputation. Character is what God uses to gauge you, while reputation is what man uses to gauge you.

Now, many people hear this and then think that they do not have to bother about their reputation. But Christ wanted us to be interested in our reputation, because if we have a bad reputation, our efforts at evangelism will be severely limited.

In John 13:35, Jesus said, "By this everyone will know that you are my disciples, if you love one another." Jesus wants people to know we are His disciples because of the way we treat each other with love. That means He cares what people think about us. So you should also take care to manage your public image. And although you should never let your reputation be more important to you than your character, you should still take care of your reputation.

However, you cannot manage your character and reputation unless you grow in these four vital areas:

Self-consciousness, Self-control, Social Consciousness, and Relationship Management.

Regarding self-consciousness, consider that Satan knows your weaknesses. If he knows your weaknesses, why is it that you do not know them? Satan is already half successful when he knows you better than you know yourself. So, learn to know yourself. What are your strengths; what are your weaknesses? What is the sin that most easily besets you? You cannot grow if you do not know yourself, and you cannot know yourself if you do not know your maker. In Hosea 6:6 God says, "I want you to show love, not offer sacrifices. I want you to know me more than I want burnt offerings" (NLT).

Just as the part of the iceberg you can't see is bigger than the part you see, you have to be bigger on the inside than you are on the outside.

Many of my readers have cars. Do you value your car? The reason we value our cars is that we spent good money to buy them. If we do not value the money we spent in buying that car, we cannot value the car. (This is what we see in the case of Jacob and his polygamous household, that he preferred Joseph, and later Benjamin, over his other sons, because he loved their mother, Rachel.) For you to value anything, you need to value what produces the thing. The reason why many people do not value their time and their work is that they do not value themselves. And the reason they do not value themselves is that they do not know themselves.

In Psalm 139:14, we read: "I praise you because I am fearfully and wonderfully made; your works are wonderful, I know that full well." Did you know there is a hidden meaning to this verse? You see, if you do not know that you are fearfully and wonderfully made, you can't praise God the way that David wrote about.

People who do not have self-control always want to control others. Do you know why? Because if we do not have self-control, then some other being is controlling us. And if a being other than God is controlling us, what is the motive of this being? The motive is to control all of humanity. So if they control you, you will find yourself trying to control others. But it is not you. The spirit within you is trying to control others.

The biggest mistake one can make is to think that the Holy Bible is a book of law. Not true. The Bible is actually a book of love. And the greatest love of all is learning to love God, and then learning to love yourself. If you do not love yourself, you can't love others.

You see, knowledge is the key to increasing in self-consciousness.

Then you move to the next step, which is self-control. Satan attacks our capacity to increase in self-control by tempting us with our besetting sins. One sure way to destroy the power of the temptation for your besetting sin is that as soon as the temptation comes, you discipline yourself to think of the consequences of the sin rather than the pleasure in the sin.

Another way that we can focus our minds away from temptation is to think of the rewards of delayed gratification. The Enemy tempts us to put our trust in money and material things. Do not trust in the provision (money and material things); rather, put your trust in the provider. All provision is created and instituted by God. "They exchanged the truth about God for a lie, and worshiped and served created things rather than the Creator—who is forever praised. Amen" (Romans 1:25).

One definition of wisdom is: the reward for surviving the temptation the Enemy brings your way. As we grow in self-control, we grow in wisdom leading to the next stage in our development.

We need to grow in Social Consciousness. If we do not really know and understand ourselves to a very high degree, we can't really empathize with others. And if we can't empathize with others, we will be limited in social awareness. And let me just say, empathy is a big word that means being able to put ourselves in another person's shoes. Now, if we cannot even put ourselves in our own shoes, what are the chances that we can put ourselves in another man's shoes? Very little!

In Philippians 2:4 introduces us to relationship management when it exhorts us as follows: "Not looking to your own interests but each of you to the interests of the others." Do you know that we cannot even be successful in business if we do not apply this principle? We can't be wrapped up in ourselves and expect to be successful in business, which requires us to provide a needed product or service to consumers. If you can't empathize, go on and become a model or some other profession where you can thrive by beautifying yourself and getting others attracted to you. But be careful, that will only last as long as you are young.

True success comes from understanding God so that you can understand yourself, and so you can understand others. Consider that even in the secular world, a successful businessperson focuses on the needs of his customers and not his own needs, and he is thus better able to serve them. In serving them, he makes a profit.

Jesus taught us the way to success in anything in life. Unfortunately, because this teaching does not involve spiritual things (like laying on of hands and giving of double anointing), we have omitted doing what Christ said while the world has stolen it.

Look at what Christ said is the secret to success. Let us read Luke 22:24-27:

A dispute also arose among them as to which of them was considered to be greatest. Jesus said to them, "The kings of the Gentiles lord it over them; and those who exercise author-ity over them call themselves Benefactors. But you are not to be like that. Instead, the greatest among you should be like the youngest, and the one who rules like the one who serves. For who is greater, the one who is at the table or the one who serves? Is it not the one who is at the table? But I am among you as one who serves."

Now to understand what Jesus meant in verse 27, we need to consider Philippians 2:5: "Let this mind be in you, which was also in Christ Jesus." Let this mind. What mind? The mind He displayed in Luke 22:27.

Incidentally, most people like go-getters. There is just something attractive about them. The reason why there are so few go-getters and so many who would want to be go-getters but are not is that the crowd sees the glamour of the go-getter, but they do not see the preparation.

You can't be a go-getter without first being a "go-giver." You always get more of what you give. Give the ground seed and you get a harvest. Those who live by the principle of Luke 6:38 are the go-getters that stay getting.

This is an issue today. A church is not a business, and if the motivation for opening or expanding a church is driven by an entrepreneurial spirit rather than a desire to save the lost, what we will end up with will be churches without depth, whose messages are specifically tailored not to offend people, but to please them and render them more willing to give.

Highbrow areas are not the only harvest field Jesus talked about. High poverty areas are, in fact, the areas where Jesus spent most of His time on earth. Hebrews 12:2 urges us to look unto Jesus, "the author and finisher of our faith." Many people were often excited and ecstatic when Jesus healed, performed miracles, and blessed people. But EVERY TIME Jesus preached to people, there were ONLY three reactions: 1) People were convicted of sins, 2) People were convicted and offended and 3) People were convicted, offended, and then plotted to kill Him. If all you ever hear is a feel-good message, then is it possible that the preaching is not confronting the imperfections in you? Remember what Jesus said, in Luke 6:26: "Woe unto you, when all men shall speak well of you! for so did their fathers to the false prophets."

Individually, we should also check ourselves that we have not become Laodiceans who have lost touch with our spiritual side and fail to discern that we have become deadened to God's pleasure because of the message of the feel-good gospel.

The reason it is very important and even necessary to grow on earth is because life on earth isn't really life. It is the preparation for life. In Matthew 18:8 Jesus said, "If your hand or your foot causes you to stumble, cut it off and throw it away. It is better for you to enter life maimed or crippled than to have two hands or two feet and be thrown into eternal fire." If this life were the only life, why would Jesus say it is better for you to enter into life?

Humans are like books. Our First Edition (life on earth) isn't perfect. But depending on your publisher, the Second Edition (life eternal) can be a corrected edition. As an author, I've met writers who complained that pirates have hijacked their books and so they didn't make any money from their intellectual property. That is a metaphor for what happens with life. The Devil is a pirate that steals God's intellectual property, which we are. If you let him, he will hijack your life and deprive you of the benefits that God, who is our Publisher, intended for us. And once you die as a pirated book, which publisher will like to give you a Second Edition? The only way to be sure of a Second Edition in Christ is to make Jesus your Lord and personal Savior. Jesus said, "The thief comes not, but to steal, and to kill, and to destroy: I am come that they might have life, and that they might have it more abundantly." The life He refers to here is the Second corrected Edition.

Forget about how much money you are depositing in the banks of earth and ask yourself: what am I depositing in the bank of heaven? "For where your treasure is, there your heart will be also" (Matthew 6:21).

HOW TO GET PROMOTED

In the previous chapter, I wrote that life on earth is the first edition of our book and a second edition of our book is the eternal life we will get if we are worthy. This process of promotion is important both here and in the life to come, because as Proverbs 4:18 teaches us, God's desire for us is that we grow in a continuum of maturity that leads to promotion.

So first, how do we get promoted on earth? In Numbers 27:16-19 we see the reason God promoted Joshua:

May the Lord, the God who gives breath to all living things, appoint someone over this community to go out and come in before them, one who will lead them out and bring them in, so the Lord's people will not be like sheep without a shepherd. So the Lord said to Moses, "Take Joshua son of Nun, a man in whom is the spirit of leadership, and lay your hand on him. Have him stand before Eleazar the priest and the entire assembly and commission him in their presence."

Joshua had the Spirit in him, and this marked him for promotion.

From Psalm 75:6-7, we understand that God is the judge of all promotions on earth, and in promoting Joshua, we see the yardstick He used: Joshua had the Spirit. "For promotion comes neither from the east, nor from the west, nor from the south. But God is the judge: he puts down one, and sets up another" (NKJV).

Now Joshua was not born with the Spirit. The Holy Spirit indwelled him during the course of his life. How did Joshua develop the Spirit? In Joshua 1:8, he tells us how: "Keep this Book of the Law always on your lips; meditate on it day and night, so that you may be careful to do everything written in it. Then you will be prosperous and successful."

Jesus corroborated Joshua in John 6:63 saying, "The Spirit gives life; the flesh counts for nothing. The words I have spoken to you—they are full of the Spirit and life."

From the above, it is clear that the more we read the words of God and His Son, Jesus, and then meditate on them, the more we are indwelled by the Spirit and the higher we will be promoted.

Some may ask, what about ungodly people who are promoted? Why are they promoted?

In Exodus 9:16, God said of Pharaoh: "But I have raised you up for this very purpose, that I might show you my power and that my name might be proclaimed in all the earth." From this verse, we see that God promoted the pharaoh of Moses' day so that He could destroy him, and in doing so demonstrated His supremacy over the affairs of men.

In 2 Kings 21:8-9 we read: "I will not again make the feet of the Israelites wander from the land I gave their ancestors, if only they will be careful to do everything I commanded them and will keep the whole Law that my servant Moses gave them. But the people did not listen. Manasseh led them astray, so that they did more evil than the nations the LORD had destroyed before the Israelites."

We see from this Scripture that when a nation or a people forsake God, God can permit rulers who will lead them to their destruction as a punishment, as well as a means of causing them pain, so they can return to Him upon repentance.

God's ideal is for the righteous to rule, but God will not interfere with human will. So, there are occasions that God will raise or permit a non-righteous ruler to emerge as a means of destroying the plan of the Enemy or punishing a people who have rejected Him.

Moreover, the righteous will not rule simply because they are righteous. They have to prepare themselves for leadership by imbibing the Word of God and increasing the indwelling of the Spirit in them.

Thus, in Proverbs 29:2, King Solomon says: "When the righteous are in authority, the people rejoice: but when the wicked bears rule, the people mourn" (NKJV). The use of the word "when" in this verse is instructive. It indicates that the righteous will rule when they are ready to rule. But if they are not ready, the wicked will rule, because nature abhors a vacuum.

Plato said, "The price good men pay for indifference to public affairs is to be ruled by evil men." This is so true. Plato reiterated a universal principle established by the True and Living God of the Bible, through His Son, in Matthew 5:14-16: "You are the light of the world. A town built on a hill cannot be hidden. Neither do people light a lamp and put it under a bowl. Instead they put it on its stand, and it gives light to everyone in the house. In the same way, let your light shine before others, that they may see your good deeds and glorify your Father in heaven."

Jesus said, "You are the light of the world." If the lights of this world, which are you and I, refuse to shine, then what will happen? Of course, darkness will take over.

If you are looking for promotion in any area of your life, do not go after it the natural way by showing off and competing with your rivals. No! Feed the Spirit in you by imbibing the Word of God, and let the Spirit begin to lead you. Before long, you will be promoted.

This was the case with Daniel as we see in Daniel 6:3: "Then this Daniel was preferred above the presidents and satraps, because an excellent spirit was in him; and the king thought to set him over the whole realm." The reason why Daniel was preferred above everybody else in Babylon was because of the Spirit in him.

How did Daniel get that Spirit? In exactly the same way that Joshua did. Daniel 9:2 proves this: "In the first year of his reign, I, Daniel, understood from the Scriptures, according to the word of the LORD given to Jeremiah the prophet, that the desolation of Jerusalem would last seventy years." Daniel's understanding came from reading the Bible.

Nobody can stop a man from rising who is increasing in the indwelling of the Spirit.

In Revelations 3:15-16 we read, "I know your deeds, that you are neither cold nor hot. I wish you were either one or the other! So, because you are lukewarm—neither hot nor cold—I am about to spit you out of my mouth." Jesus here says He prefers us to be hot.

Many times in the Bible, the Holy Spirit is depicted as air or wind. We see this in John 3:8: "The wind blows wherever it pleases. You hear its sound, but you cannot tell where it comes from or where it is going. So it is with everyone born of the Spirit." In John 20:22 we also read that Jesus "breathed on them and said, 'Receive the Holy Spirit.'"

Now that we have established that the Holy Spirit is depicted as air, and Jesus desires that we be hot, let us ask ourselves what happens when air is hot? It rises. When we are hot with the Holy Spirit, we will rise in life.

Human beings are not the judge of who will be promoted. When God wants to promote you, events will orchestrate themselves such that you may think that a human being is behind it. This precept is established in Daniel 4:32: "You will be driven away from people and will live with the wild animals; you will eat grass like the ox. Seven times will pass by for you until you acknowledge that the Most High is sovereign over all kingdoms on earth and gives them to anyone he wishes" (Daniel 4:32).

Some of us Christians are complaining that we are being treated like animals where we work. It may be that we are receiving that treatment because we are yet to acknowledge "that the Most High is sovereign over all kingdoms on earth and gives them to anyone he wishes."

Some may think, that is not me. But when we prioritize the things of our boss over the things of God, what are we telling God?

Daniel was faithful and competent in his job, but he never prioritized it over God, and as such, God ensured that he was preferred above those who did otherwise. He was an important man—the most important man in all of Babylon. Yet we read: "When Daniel learned that the decree had been published, he went home to his upstairs room where the windows opened toward Jerusalem. Three times a day he got down on his knees and prayed, giving thanks to his God, just as he had done before" (Daniel 6:10). Note the words "just as he had done before." This means that it was his usual custom to pray three times a day, irrespective of who was waiting on him at the office!

Ephesians 6:6-8 gives the same recipe for promotion as Psalm 75:6-7 saying, "obey them not only to win their favor when their eye is on you, but as slaves of Christ, doing the will of God from your heart. Serve wholeheartedly, as if you were serving the Lord, not people, because you know that the Lord will reward each one for whatever good they do, whether they are slave or free." God is the promoter, not man! It may seem like it is a man doing it, but God orchestrated His actions.

One of the most consistent prayers people offer is to pray to God to meet all their needs. It is such a widespread prayer request that Jesus included it in the Lord's Prayer in Matthew 6:11.

However, if you really want God to meet you at the point of your need, ask yourself if you are a faithful person. In Luke 16:11, Jesus said, "If you have not been trustworthy in handling worldly wealth, who will trust you with true riches?"

One of the greatest principles in the handling of money is to understand that God has promised to give bread to the eater and seed to the sower. Isaiah 55:10: "As the rain and the snow come down from heaven, and do not return to it without watering the earth and making it bud and flourish, so that it yields seed for the sower and bread for the eater."

This principle works irrespective of a person's state of salvation.

When we understand this principle, we will understand what the Bible means when it says that "for certainly money maketh wings for itself and flies" (Proverbs 23:5).

This agrees with Ecclesiastes 2:26, which says "to the person who pleases him, God gives wisdom, knowledge and happiness, but to the sinner he gives the task of gathering and storing up wealth to hand it over to the one who pleases God. This too is meaningless, a chasing after the wind."

In this world, there are only two types of people. There are eaters who get bread and there are sowers who get seed. Every time money gets into the hands of a person with an "eater" mentality, the principle in Proverbs 23:5 operates. Money leaves that person's hands and flies back to heaven, where it is redirected to the hands of the person with a "sower" mentality.

This is what the Bible means in Proverbs 11:24 when it says that one withholds more than it is right, and comes to poverty, while another gives out more and comes to wealth.

If you look at the world, there is a pattern. The richest nations are those nations that regularly give other nations foreign aid. The poorest nations are those that regularly receive foreign aid from other nations. And as long as those nations continue to receive from rich nations, they can never be rich themselves, because spiritually they are providing the platform for those rich nations to keep getting richer. Hence, the worldly maxim: the richer get richer and the poor get poorer. The truth is, by an application of the principle God set out in Genesis 8:22, which says, "While the earth remains, seedtime and harvest, cold and heat, summer and winter, day and night, shall not cease," those who give will continue to receive. This is a natural principle that you cannot bypass, and it is corroborated by Proverbs 11:24: "One man gives freely, yet gains even more; another withholds unduly, but comes to poverty."

If you try to bypass it, you will only break yourself.

CONSTANTLY RENEWING YOUR WHOLE MIND

Have you ever handled a remote control toy? I bought a remote controlled helicopter for my twin boys. The remote control flies the helicopter anywhere you want it to go. It is so cool. But just like the remote controlled helicopter, humanity is controlled by spirit beings using the remote control of suggestions to our minds, which many people believe are their own original thoughts. The only difference is that the physical remote control is obvious, because it is a slow motion version of the spiritual remote control.

Jeremiah 10:23 tells us: "O LORD, I know that the way of man is not in himself: it is not in man who walks to direct his steps" (NKJV). Our lives do not even belong to us. The only reason why we will give an account of our lives at the end is because it is God's life, which He gives us by breathing into our mortal body the breath of life. Think about, if you have money that belongs to you, would you have to give an account of it to your boss? No. But if your boss gives you money, you must of necessity account for it.

Thoughts are the remote control of the spiritual realm. God guides us using thoughts, and we see that principle in Jeremiah 29:11: "For I know the thoughts that I think toward you, says the LORD, thoughts of peace, and not of evil, to give you an expected end" (NKJV).

I worked in the Silicon Valley for four years, and I know that websites are held up by code. Ask any techie in the Silicon Valley, and he or she will tell you that every good website is a magnet for hackers. They want to hack it so they can gain control of the site.

The whole of creation is God's website. God wants to guide us with the codes that He used to form creation, which is why He gave us the Bible. In Matthew 16:19, Jesus said, "I will give you the keys of the kingdom of heaven; whatever you bind on earth will be bound in heaven, and whatever you loose on earth will be loosed in heaven." How did Jesus give Peter the keys to the kingdom? The keys to the kingdom are the principles that Jesus taught. They are the codes, the program that God used in creating creation. That is why Jesus said in Luke 17:21 that "the kingdom of God is within you." But let me ask you, if you are not reading the Word of God on a regular basis, then how can the Kingdom of God be within you?

In Deuteronomy 11:18, God gave us the secrets to the keys of the kingdom when speaking through Moses. He said, "Fix these words of mine in your hearts and minds; tie them as symbols on your hands and bind them on your foreheads."

In 2 Timothy 3:16-17, God revealed His intention for giving us the Word: so that we will be perfect, lacking nothing.

Have you ever had the experience of going to a computer and typing in a command, or perhaps pulling up the browser and typing in a website, and the computer shows you an hourglass or something spinning which indicates that it is thinking? Then after a few seconds or microseconds, the website that you wanted manifests or the command you have given it is obeyed?

You see, that is why God gave you a mind. If you fill up your mind with the Word of God, anytime you have a challenge or an issue, your mind will begin to scan the Word of God that you have committed to it (just like the computer's "thinking" is represented by the hourglass), and from that bank of stored Word a solution to your issue will manifest.

The worst advice that you can ever give to anybody is to say, "Just follow your heart." Follow your principles, not your heart. "The heart is deceitful above all things, and desperately wicked" (Jeremiah 17:9). Would you deliberately take advice from a wicked person? Not likely. Especially if you have foreknowledge of the person's wickedness. So if that is the case, why would you follow the adage that says "listen to your heart"?

You are not meant to listen to yourself; you are meant to talk to yourself. Your heart is the seat of your inner self. If your listen to it, you will become selfish and self-centered. You will also surrender control to the self. But if you talk to yourself, you will become selfless and others-centered, which will catapult you into leadership.

In Matthew 15:19, Yeshu'a says, "Out of the heart proceed evil thoughts, murders, adulteries, fornications, thefts, false witness, blasphemies." Guess what will happen if you listen to your heart? You will begin to do those things listed above. The best athletes and soldiers are taught not to listen to their self before attempting difficult tasks, because it will discourage them. Instead they are told to psych themselves by speaking to it.

Don't believe what your heart tells you. Believe what the Word of God tells you, then psyche your heart to believe it too. Psyche your heart; don't be psyched by it.

Luke 6:45 says, "A good man brings good things out of the good stored up in his heart, and an evil man brings evil things out of the evil stored up in his heart. For the mouth speaks what the heart is full of." From this verse, we see that what you store up in your heart is what you will bring out. If you have not stored up godly principles in your heart, then what your heart will bring out will be toxic to you.

I talked about hackers previously. Hackers are very creative. The operating system that man was made to function with is the Word of God. We see this clearly in Deuteronomy 8:3: "Man does not live on bread alone but on every word that comes from the mouth of the LORD."

Similarly, in 1 John 5:19 we read: "We know that we are children of God, and that the whole world is under the control of the evil one."

Many people, either because of their backgrounds or because of deliberate disinformation by the Enemy, believe that the way the devil controls the world is by some magical spiritual power. No! That idea represents lower level demonic activity—low hanging fruits in the kingdom of darkness.

The devil operates under the principle: as the mind goes so goes the man. And so, he is very practical.

In Revelations 11:15, the seventh angel said, "The kingdom of the world has become the kingdom of our Lord and of his Messiah, and he will reign for ever and ever." From this verse, we understand that in the future, the kingdoms of this world will become the kingdoms of God and Jesus. If that is the case, whose are they now?

Of course, we know that the devil offered up the powers of this world to Jesus in Matthew 4:8-9. That means, for the time being, the powers of this world are his to control. Let us examine this concept further.

Every year, Forbes publishes a list of the world's richest people and another list of the world's most powerful people. One man who regular features in the top fifty most powerful people is Rupert Murdock. Rupert Murdock does not hold any political office; he does not command any army. Then why is he probably the most regularly featured man on the Forbes list of the world's most powerful people?

Because he controls more of the world's media than any other single human being. He is the CEO of Newscorp. If you watch news, he influences you through his company, Sky Broadcasting. If you read newspapers, he influences you through his chains of newspapers all over the world, such as The Wall Street Journal, The Times of London, and the Sun. If you read books, he influences you through his company, HarperCollins. If you watch movies, he influences you through his company, Twentieth Century Fox.

So, you can see that whoever controls the media controls the power of this world, and whoever controls the man that controls the media controls the power he wields.

You see, the devil is very practical when it comes to hacking the minds of humans, and he is successful because humans, who are looking for him to be magical about it, do not recognize his tactics.

Good websites are built with enough capacity to withstand hackers. And hacking literally works when the intruder's codes overwrite the owner's codes. The only reason your inner man will be hacked by the Enemy's code is if you do not have enough of your Maker's code in you. An insufficiency of the Maker's code will open the firewall, so that with very little effort, the Enemy can over write your code.

It is impossible to function in this world without reading or hearing or watching the media. That means that you are always at threat from hackers. Thus, the only way you can safeguard your mind is by regularly replenishing it with the Word of God.

Let us learn from the Scriptures the strategy the devil uses to wear us down and break our defenses so that we succumb to him. In Luke 18:5, Jesus spoke a parable that ended with the heartless judge saying, "Because this widow keeps bothering me, I will see that she gets justice, so that she won't eventually come and attack me!" Jesus is telling us here that almost anyone can be cracked with persistence. The devil is very persistent, and the only way to defeat him in the battle for our minds is to wear him out.

Although Satan is talkative, he is also a gradualist. He does not just tempt us to conform in a 180-degree turn. No! He turns the gear gradually. What you see affects what you think about. And what you think about affects who you really are!

David was called a man after God's heart, and we see one of the reasons why in Psalm 16:8 when he said that he cannot be moved because he sets God at his right hand.

We cannot pay more attention to the world and expect that we will not conform, just as we cannot pay more attention to the Word and expect not to be transformed.

In James 4:7, we are told to "submit yourselves, then, to God. Resist the devil, and he will flee from you." Modern day Christians like the latter part of this verse because it is the lazy part. You often hear people say resist the devil and he will flee. But the only way you can resist the devil is by submitting to God.

So how do you submit to God? In Ecclesiastes 12:13, King Solomon tells us how, saying, "Fear God and keep his commandments, for this is the duty of all mankind." The only way you can submit to God is to keep His commandments, and the only way you can keep His commandments is if you know them. The only way you can know them is by constantly reading them.

Dag Hammarskjöld, a Lutheran Christian and former United Nations Secretary General, once said, "You cannot play with the animal in you without becoming wholly animal, play with falsehood without forfeiting your right to truth, play with cruelty without losing your sensitivity of mind. He who wants to keep his garden tidy does not reserve a plot for weeds."

You see brethren, if you are not renewing your mind with the Word of God on a daily basis, you are reserving a plot in your mind for weeds. "He also that received seed among the thorns is he that hears the word; and the care of this world, and the deceitfulness of riches, choke the word, and he becomes unfruitful" (Matthew 13:22).

The cares of this world is the manufactured reality that the media serves to us. Some may say that is not true; that Jesus in that verse is talking about material riches and wealth. But consider that if the media was not flashing ads of the latest fashion, the latest cars, the latest gadget, how would the manufacturers of those products be able to fill us up with desire to buy the things we do not need, to such an extent that our lives now revolve around looking for money to buy things that will cease to be fashionable the minute we buy it? Using the same principle, if we are not constantly flashing the

Word of God in our mind, how can we "buy the truth, and sell it not" (Proverbs 12:23)?

Are you aware that before the media advertises this year's fashion, cars, movies and gadgets, the manufacturers of those products are already working on next year's version? This whole process is the choking of the Word that is referred to in Matthew 13:22.

Ask yourself this question: who is more important to this world--a genuine man of God, a professional athlete, an actor, or a pop singer? Now ask yourself why is it that if an athlete, an actor, or a pop singer buys a new jet, the purchase is not the subject of outrage by the media. In fact, the media will celebrate it. But if a man of God gets one legitimately and for spreading the Gospel, it becomes a subject of outrage in the media.

Let me tell you the main purpose of the media. You see, the devil knows that human beings have two minds—a conscious mind and an unconscious mind.

Have you ever been driving somewhere and you get lost in thought, and then you arrive at your destination, and suddenly you become more conscious of yourself, realizing that you drove there without consciously thinking about what you were doing because of the issue that was occupying your mind?

At that moment, you were utilizing your unconscious mind.

Some experts have estimated that the average human being uses his conscious mind only 5 percent of the time. In 95 percent of the time, the unconscious mind is in control!

But what fuels the unconscious mind? Everything that you see, hear, touch, feel, and taste. Subliminally, you are being controlled by the totality of your experiences on earth that your mind has filed away.

Let me explain it like this. Though many of us have computers, we are, largely, unaware that every document we write on our computer remains in the memory of that computer. When we delete the document, it never really deletes. It is compressed and sent to a recycle bin where it stays hidden from view to us, but it is still there. A computer technician can access every document that we think we have deleted.

In the same way, every experience we have had from childhood, including the ones that we have forgotten, are stored in our unconscious mind. When we forget it, it has the same effect as a man deleting a document from a computer. All that happens is that it goes from our conscious memory to our unconscious memory.

Every time we do not consciously make a decision based on our new set of Christian principles (that we are aware of), we unconsciously take a decision from our forgotten principles that have been consigned to our unconscious mind.

Now, most of those experiences in our unconscious mind are experiences that were influenced by the media. That horror film you watched when you were five years old has an effect on why some things scare you as an adult. That neighbor who watched his parents having intimate relations and then came to "practice" with you as a six year old, has an effect on why you are today attracted to (or terrified of) a particular kind of person or behaviors.

All these experiences are, in one way or the other, linked to the media. And, you see, the origin of the media goes back to Genesis 3:1-6:

Now the serpent was more crafty than any of the wild animals the Lord God had made. He said to the woman, "Did God really say, 'You must not eat from any tree in the garden'?" The woman said to the serpent, "We may eat fruit from the trees in the garden, but God did say, 'You must not eat fruit from the tree that is in the middle of the garden, and you must not touch it, or you will die.'" "You will not certainly die," the serpent said to the woman. "For God knows that when you eat from it your eyes will be opened, and you will be like God, knowing good and evil." When the woman saw that the fruit of the tree was good for food and pleasing to the eye, and also desirable for gaining wisdom, she took some and ate it. She also gave some to her husband, who was with her, and he ate it.

All that the media has been doing from that time until today is to put suggestions into your mind that run contrary to God's commandments. This is the true meaning of 1 John 5:19: "The whole world is under the control of the evil one."

Satan knows that if he tells you to wear some sexually provocative clothes, you will not wear them. So he goes to the media, and they select the most beautiful or handsome celebrity and pay them money to wear clothes that even they would not have worn in ordinary circumstances. But because of the money, they wear it. Then they put these pictures in magazines, on movies, in the news and newspapers. And the next month, your best friend if wearing it. The month after that you cousin is wearing it. The week after it is your sister. Finally, you yourself wear it.

You see, by patiently using the media to orchestrate his plans, Satan has gotten you to do what he would not have been able to get you to do by direct control. In other words, where direct control fails, remote controlling works.

At this point, let us read Jeremiah 10:23 again. "O LORD, I know that the way of man is not in himself: it is not in man who walks to direct his steps."

You only think you are in control of your life. But if you have not handed your life over to Jesus, then as surely as you are reading this, the devil is in control of your life. It may not be direct control, as is the case with occultists and people who sell their souls to him; but he will surely get the unsaved by remote control.

This is the principle used in advertising. This is the principle used in music. Most of the time when you are humming a song aloud, it was not your conscious mind that recalled that song. Rather, your unconscious mind summoned that song, your conscious mind accepted the command, and you started humming. That is why at times you will say, how did that song just pop into my mind or my head?

This is what God means in Romans 12:2 when He says we should renew our minds. He is not so much as talking about our conscious minds as He is talking about our unconscious minds.

Have you ever asked yourself why the Gospel is sometimes referred to as the "good news"? Because it runs contrary to the world and the artificial reality created by the media. The Bible is good news! Consider that in the world's news, the first priority is that if it is bad news put it in the front pages of the newspaper. The media deliberately suppresses good news and amplifies bad news. If you doubt me, go home, put on CNN, and take an inventory of the type news that they broadcast. Take good news to a top newspaper or TV station and they will tell you that it is not newsworthy because it is not bad news.

In 2005, Andy Roddick and Fernando Verdasco played tennis at the Rome Masters in Rome, Italy. Roddick was on the verge of winning the game, but he started complaining and the match officials went to meet with him to ask him what the issue was. He said that the ball that his opponent played, and which the lines man claimed was out, was not really out and that the linesman and the umpire had cheated his opponent. The opponent did not complain, but Andy Roddick complained for him. They went back, checked the play, and found that Roddick was right. So they asked Fernando Verdasco to retake the play, which he did, and came back from defeat to win that game.

Do you know the headline that CNN carried the next day? "Honesty Backfires as Roddick Loses." Do you see how the world reasons? The world thinks of the now, but Christians have to think of eternity. Roddick lost in that present time because "the whole world is under the control of the evil one." But Roddick gained in eternity.

When a broadcasting station is planning a particular program, they will remind their audience that this program will air on such and such a date. Sometimes we often ask each other, when will that program air? Or, has it aired? Every time we hear or use that word, we are using it in a biblical sense, only we are not conscious of it.

In Ephesians 2:2 we read: "In which in time past you walked according to the course of this world, according to the prince of the power of the air, the spirit that now works in the children of disobedience" (NKJV). Ponder on that statement. Chew it over in your minds. What is the power of the air that the devil has which makes Scripture call him "the prince of the power of the air"?

In addition, it is not just secular things that the media puts into our subconscious. The media is even manipulating the church.

There are many things that we do in the church that have no origins in the Bible, but we practice them, and the media is used to burning them into our subconscious until we accept that these things are in the Bible when they are not.

Let us read Deuteronomy 6:25. From this verse, we understand that God wants us to worship Him in the way He prescribes. You are righteous when you obey God the way He asks you to obey Him.

One day my mother was having a discussion with me, and she mentioned how the three wise men visited the baby Jesus on Christmas. I told my mother that there is no such story in the Bible. Well, you know a Nigerian mother—she told me, "Shut up, who taught you Bible, is it not me"?

I then had her open the Bible, and at age seventy-eight, for the first time in her life, my mother, who reads the Bible every day, discovered that Jesus was not born at Christmas, that there weren't three wise men, but a group of Magi from the East, and that Jesus was two years old when they visited Him.

She then told me, that if I had not shown this to her in Scripture, she would have been sure that she had read all these things in Scripture. I then explained to my mother that it was the media that subtly corrupts the Bible by adding and subtracting to it through movies, advertising, music, etc. all to promote the Satanic agenda.

Twice in Scripture we are told of the mind of Christ. Philippians 2:5 says, "Let this mind be in you which was in Christ Jesus," and 1 Corinthians 2:16 says that we have the "mind of Christ."

When we realize the depth of scripting that the Enemy has performed on us with the media, we will begin to realize that just a perfunctory reading of the Word of God is not enough to renew our minds, especially our conscious minds.

I previously dwelt on how every item that is deleted is retained in our computers. However, you can get a computer technician to wipe them out. It is this wiping out that God refers to in Romans 12:2: "Be not conformed to this world: but be transformed by the renewing of your mind." But you cannot wipe out what the media has imprinted into your mind if you spend more time feeding your conscious mind with the media's diet than with the Word of God.

What happens is that the world is entering you at a faster pace than the Word is entering you. Do you know what will happen to you if you are like that? Matthew 13:22 says the world will choke the Word and it will become unfruitful in you. The thorns and the cares of this world are shows like Meet the Kardashians, The Real Housewives of Atlanta, European Premiership League, fashion, flashy cars, March Madness. In short, anything that competes with the Word of God for your time and money are "the cares of this world." and they are fed to you principally using the media.

When Jesus says in John 7:38 that if anyone believes in Him, out of his belly shall flow rivers of living waters, He is not talking about a literal belly, and He is not referring to literal water. In fact, the New International Version does not use the term belly. It says "living water will flow from within him."

The within that Jesus is referring to is our mind, and specifically, our subconscious mind. He means that we will be full to overflowing with the water, which is a metaphor for the Word of God, and we will be so full that the Living Water shall flow from within us. It will so permeate our subconscious that it will form the paradigm through which we see the world.

My wife's brother has diabetes, and I often see him calculating the carbohydrates in every food that he eats so that he does not have too much sugar in his blood. If he has too much sugar, he stands the risk of death. I learned something from him.

If the Holy Spirit has convicted you with this message, try to do this exercise: Get a journal, and every night before you sleep, write down the amount of time you spent in that day on thinking about the things of the world. Also write how much time you devoted to thinking about the things of God. If your meditation is more on the world than on the Word, then you may be at risk for spiritual diabetes.

The cure for spiritual diabetes is to take in the medicine of the Word more than you take in the message of the world.

UNDERSTANDING YOUR CREATIVE ABILITIES

In Acts 12:7, we read where the chains that had been used to bind Peter's hands fell off without any physical or spiritual activity of the angel that was sent to deliver him. The only thing that the angel did was speak.

The Body of Christ has underestimated the value and importance of words. Before they became agents of communication, words were intended as creative agents. In Genesis chapter 1, from verse 1 to 25, every time God spoke, it was to create a part of this world. He said, "Let there be" seven times in the first twenty-five verses. Each time, His words created something material and tangible. It was not until verse 26 that we see God using words to converse. He said, "Let us make mankind in our image, in our likeness." This should tell you that you are "like" God and, therefore, not merely communicating when you speak. In fact, when you speak, you are creating your experiences.

Your problems in life are not the work of an enemy. They are the result of your own words. When you become aware of the potency of your words, even your enemy will be at peace with you.

In Acts 12:10 (NKJV), we read further that Peter and the angel "came unto the iron gate that leads unto the city; which opened to them of its own accord." Notice from this verse that even a gate of iron has a will of its own, because we see that the verse says, "which opened to them of its own accord."

From this verse, we get clarity on what Romans 8:19 means by "the creation waits in eager expectation for the children of God to be revealed."

Everything that has been created by God, whether a living thing or non-living thing, is waiting for the children of the Most High to know that they have power over them and can command them according to their desire that is in agreement to the will of God.

In Genesis 1:28, God gave man dominion over other living things and subduing powers over non-living things. That is what is meant in the words "and replenish the earth, and subdue it." You are meant to use your words to subdue non-living things, such as the elements. This is the hidden meaning of Romans 8:19.

Yeshu'a reiterated this power that God gave us in Mark 11:23: "If anyone says to this mountain, 'Go, throw yourself into the sea,' and does not doubt in their heart but believes that what they say will happen, it will be done for them."

Essentially, what happened after the fall of man is that humans forgot who they were and what powers they have. Yeshu'a, the Son of God, was sent to save us and remind us who we are. This is why Hebrews 12:2 says we should look unto Him. He is our example, our Mentor.

In the incident recorded in Matthew 8:26 and 27 when Yeshu'a slept while the tempest raged around the boat, Jesus expected his disciples to know that they had power over the elements (non-living things in their natural forms), which is why He rebuked them for being of little faith. Yeshu'a showed

His disciples what to do in situations when the tempest comes. He rebuked it and it obeyed Him.

An element literally means an entity that is a part of or affects the Earth, such as earth, the sun, the moon, wind, water, fire, natural minerals like iron, copper, rocks, etc.

God gave us authority over them. If you know anything about God, you know that He does not withdraw His gifts. This is established in Romans 11:29: "God's gifts and his call can never be withdrawn" (NLT).

We all can speak to elements and they will obey us. But as Yeshu'a said in Mark 11:23, we must not have doubts when speaking to them; otherwise, they will not obey.

There is a reason God said we should speak to elements but pray about people. Elements are different from humans.

When God was creating elements, He spoke them into being. This tells you that at their barest irreducible minimum, elements consist of words and therefore respond to words.

Let me explain deeper. A diamond is one of the hardest substances known to man. If you want to cut diamonds, you cannot use iron or gold because they will break. Diamonds only respond to diamonds. They cannot be cut by lesser elements.

Now, take elements as something that may need cutting, stopping, or one form of adjustment or another. Just as only diamond can cut diamond, the only thing that can perform that adjustment is an element that has equal or greater power than the element you are trying to adjust.

What did Yeshu'a say we should do to elements in Mark 11:23? He said we should speak to them and they will obey us. But only if we do not doubt in our heart.

Notice the key thing—in our heart. It is not what you say that matters, but what you believe.

In Joshua 10:12 and 13, Joshua spoke to the sun and the moon and they obeyed him. "Joshua said to the LORD in the presence of Israel: 'Sun, stand still over Gibeon, and you, moon, over the Valley of Aijalon.' So the sun stood still, and the moon stopped." Do you see what Joshua did? He said to the sun and the moon, "stand still," and they obeyed his word.

Now, your spirit man is not material and has no physical matter in it, however, your body and environments are elemental. Your words do not originate from your body. It is your spirit that originates the words your mouth enunciates. This is the reason man is the only creature on earth that can originate words, because man is the only creature with a spirit.

God's intention is that we are to be co-creators with Him.

So, every word that you speak has an effect on your body and your environment.

That is why Proverbs 13:2 says, "A man shall eat good by the fruit of his mouth."

You need to understand that whereas God spoke the elements into being and created animals, the only time we read that God created anything by hand is when He created man: "Then the LORD God formed a man from the dust of the ground" (Genesis 2:7).

In the natural, when things are mass-produced by a manufacturing process, they will have value, but their value can never be the same as things that are made by hand.

That is why most times, when you see a very expensive item of clothing and you check the label, it reads Hand Made.

You and I are hand made by God, and we hold so much more value than the elements and animals and all that comes from the elements, such as money and wealth. This is why it is so displeasing to God when we spend our lives focused on wealth and other material things. When we do that, we are just like a man who sells a handmade suit in order to acquire a cheap, machine-made suit.

We should not be slave to material things; material things should be slaves to us.

For example, you can speak to situations and they will turn around for you. We are not to go according to the elements of this world. The elements of this world are to go according to us. "See to it that no one takes you captive through hollow and deceptive philosophy, which depends on human tradition and the elemental spiritual forces of this world rather than on Christ" (Colossians 2:8 NIV).

The thing to understand is that even when God commands a person, it is not always that He speaks directly to that person. His commands are implemented by elements. What happens is that His commands to a person are manifested through the elements behaving in a way that makes the human obey the command of God.

In the account of the widow of Zarephath and Elijah in1 King 17:9-14, you will notice in verse 9 that God said, "Go at once to Zarephath in the region of Sidon and stay there. I have directed a widow there to supply you with food." Though God had commanded this widow, she was oblivious of God's commands. Yet, in her ignorance, elementary things in her environment put her in a position where she could use her will to obey God's commandment without knowing she was doing so.

The thing to do now is to consciously work with the elements according to the power of God and His will. Remember, though, that this will be an exercise in futility if you have doubts in your heart. Your imaginations, thoughts, and ideas are spiritual. To manifest them in the natural, you have to condense these spiritual gifts to a dense state. I will explain.

Water is made out of the gases hydrogen and oxygen in the chemical formulae H_2O. Both hydrogen and oxygen are unseen, but by a process of condensation, the molecules that make up these two elements get denser and denser until they manifest as water, which has the capability to be seen and touched.

The way you condense imaginations, thoughts, and ideas is to keep thinking about them. Thinking about things attracts the physical manifestation of those things, which is why we often think of a person and then we see them or they call and we say, "I was just thinking about you."

When you meditate on positive imaginations, thoughts, and ideas, your natural eye will be more aware of tools and ingredients within your reach that can be combined together to manifest your vision, just like hydrogen and oxygen combine together to form water.

With this in mind, imagine and think of only what you want to happen, not what you do not want to happen. Your thoughts are the foundation for everything that you are now.

No one accidentally becomes a success in life and without a vision for where he or she wants to go. You cannot have and realize an accurate vision of success if you are constantly turning your attention to opposing pictures in your mind and out of your mind. Feed your mind with words and images that fixate it on where you want to be, and starve it of images of where you do not want to be. Set a picture of what you want from life before yourself and stick to it, irrespective of what you see. After all, we are meant to walk by faith, not by sight.

THE ENEMY IN ME

In my time in ministry, I have seen many of our brethren in the Body of Christ devoting so much negative energy to their enemies, and I am certain, deep down in my spirit man, that this does not give glory to God.

Matthew 5:14 teaches us that we are the light of the world. In verses 44 and 45, Jesus gives us a direct instruction on how we should relate to enemies. "I say unto you, love your enemies, bless them that curse you, do good to them that hate you, and pray for them which despitefully use you, and persecute you; That ye may be the children of your Father which is in heaven: for he maketh his sun to rise on the evil and on the good, and sendeth rain on the just and on the unjust."

In Acts 24:16, Paul teaches that the ideal state of the human heart is a conscience that is free from offences with God and men. Having a clear conscience does not only come from asking God for forgiveness. If you maintain a grudge against another person, your conscience cannot be clear.

According to Matthew 22:37-40, the most important spiritual laws are that we first love God, and then that we love each other. Jesus said: "'Love the Lord your God with all your heart and with all your soul and with all your mind.' This is the first and greatest commandment. And the second is like it:

'Love your neighbor as yourself.' All the Law and the Prophets hang on these two commandments."

Now notice that Yeshu'a says all other laws hang on these two laws. The problem with us today is that we like to keep the "hang-on" laws and forget to keep the main commandments of loving God and each other. So for instance, we want to pray, fast, give to charity, yet we do not have these two basic loves—for God and for others.

When 1 Corinthians 13:13 says "love is the greatest gift of all," what do we think it is talking about? It is referring to loving God and loving people.

It is very reflective of the age we live in when people say I love my car, I love these jeans, I love British Airways, I love this, I love that. Any sentence that has the word "love" should always end with the word "God," "me," or "you." Why? Because Jesus said, "Love the Lord your God with all your heart and with all your soul and with all your mind," and "Love your neighbor as yourself." We are to love only God, ourselves, and our neighbor. In simple words, love people, not things!

So do not even hate your enemies. Love them. Proverbs 16:7 teaches that when a man's ways pleases God, He makes his enemies be at peace with him. If you want peace, do not fight your enemies. Learn how to please God!

Grudges and friendships are like a wolf and a dog. If you nurse a wolf when it is a baby, it will bite you when it matures as an adult, but a dog will love you as a puppy and forever. Nurture friendships, not grudges.

If God has been good to you, even when you did not deserve it, what better way to exhibit His love than to be good to those who also do not deserve it?

It is not possible to retain the favor of God when you are constantly turning your attention to the person and deeds of your enemy. Isaiah 26:3 says "You will keep him in perfect peace, whose mind is stayed on you: because he trusts in you." It takes focus on God, and when I say focus, I mean concentrated attention, to attain and remain in peace and tranquility, which are states that put you in the best position for God to make absolute provision of your spiritual and material needs.

Our enemies are not the people out there who do things against us. We are the ones who are our own enemies. We just saw the verse that says when a man's ways please God He makes the man's enemies be at peace with him. From that verse, we understand that attacks from external enemies are the consequence of our internal enemy, which is the self that is not subjugated to God.

Let me explain deeper.

In Genesis 28:20-22, Jacob made a promise to God. But Jacob did not fulfill that promise. Instead of going to Bethel, Jacob went and settled in Shechem. Now notice what happened to him in Shechem. Let us read Genesis 34:1-2: "Now Dinah, the daughter Leah had borne to Jacob, went out to visit the women of the land. When Shechem son of Hamor the Hivite, the ruler of that area, saw her, he took her and raped her."

Now, it is easy to blame the rape of Jacob's daughter on Shechem, but the truth is that that incident happened because Jacob did not honor his vow to God and, therefore, was not situated at the place where he ought to be. That disrespect of his vow led to the consequence of the rape of Dinah.

Now, a less spiritual man would blame the enemy, which in this case was Shechem. But the real enemy was Jacob himself.

After the whole incident, what was God's solution? We see that in Genesis 35:1: "Then God said to Jacob, "Go up to Bethel and settle there, and build an altar there to God, who appeared to you when you were fleeing from your brother Esau."

Notice that the solution was for Jacob to fulfill his vow to God and be situated where God wanted him to be. If he had been at that place, he would not have suffered the pain of seeing his daughter defiled.

We see this same principle in 1 Kings 11:14 and then verse 23. "The LORD raised up against Solomon an adversary, Hadad the Edomite, from the royal line of Edom."

"And God raised up against Solomon another adversary, Rezon son of Eliada, who had fled from his master, Hadadezer king of Zobah."

This principle has not changed. And in the New Testament, we get to see a corroboration of the reason why we face afflictions and enmity.

In Matthew 28:19 Yeshu'a said, "Go and make disciples of all nations, baptizing them in the name of the Father and of the Son and of the Holy Spirit." He also repeated this instruction in Acts 1:8, saying, "You will receive power when the Holy Spirit comes on you; and you will be my witnesses in Jerusalem, and in all Judea and Samaria, and to the ends of the earth."

Here we see the precise instructions of Yeshu'a to the church. But despite hearing those instructions, the disciples and the early followers remained within their comfort zone in Jerusalem, visiting each other and congregating at the temple.

What did God do to the early Christians when they ignored His Son's instructions?

We see that in Acts 8:1 and 4: "A great persecution broke out against the church in Jerusalem, and all except the apostles were scattered throughout Judea and Samaria....Those who had been scattered preached the word wherever they went."

Do you now see the purpose for the persecution that the early Christians faced in Jerusalem? Because they refused to obey Yeshu'a's instruction to them to go to the ends of the earth for the purpose of evangelism, God stirred up enemies for them that caused them to flee Jerusalem and go to the places Jesus had asked them to go and do the very things He had asked them to do. If you do not obey God or fulfill your vows, God can allow pain in your life, because it is better for you to have pain and enter His Kingdom than to have pleasure that leads to destruction.

Many of us are in lack, in crisis, and not enjoying the John 10:10 life because we are not living in obedience to either our vows to God or God's instruction to us. God will permit afflictions to make you uncomfortable, or even unwanted, where you are, so you can leave and go to where He wants you to be.

At other times, we allow our emotions to make enemies of people who are not enemies. It is critical to understand that our emotions are indicators of how we are feeling. They should not be dictators of how we should act.

Our real enemy is the inner man that refuses to obey God. Emotions, ego, and reputation are things within and without us that we have to conquer.

Second Corinthians 4:18 says that the things which are not seen are more real than the things which are seen. This is so true on a very real level. For instance, we can see a light bulb, our furniture, and our cars. However, if we get rid of the things I listed, we would still be able to function on earth.

However, we cannot see the air around us, which consist of oxygen, carbon, and other gases. And although we cannot see them, if we were to remove the unseen gases from this world, we would all perish. In the same vein, the enemies who we cannot see are more real than the enemies we can see. Some of us even put a bar between ourselves and God and, in a sense, make God out like an enemy.

Let me go deeper.

Most people think God wants us to be afraid of Him because our Christianity has flowed from the King James Version and its translations that often say "fear God." In actuality, a closer study of the original Hebrew, Greek, and Aramaic original texts reveal that God does not want us to be afraid of Him. He wants us to revere Him. In fact, we know from 1 John 4:8 that "whoever does not love does not know God, because God is love," and 1 John 4:18 makes us understand that "perfect love casts out fear." So, how can God, who is love, wants us to be afraid of Him?

The reason is that we have been laboring under a sixteenth century translation, which defined reverence as fear. For example, The King James Version renders Exodus 20:20 thusly: "Moses said to the people, "Do not fear; for God has come to test you, and that His fear may be before you, so that you may not sin." Now, this is a contradiction if read through the eyes of modern English. It appears to be saying that God does not want you to be afraid because He wants you to be afraid. But when you read the same verse in more recent translations, it says, "Don't be afraid! God has come only to test you, so that you will be in awe of him and won't sin" (God's Word Translation).

Let me close this chapter by emphasizing that just as we have only one Father, who is the God and Father of our Lord Yeshu'a, we also have one enemy, and that is Satan, who has a kingdom of evil spiritual beings at his disposal. Please remember that "we wrestle not against flesh and blood, but against principalities, against powers, against the rulers of the darkness of this world, against spiritual wickedness in high places."

No matter how much you dislike a person, he or she is not your enemy.

UNDERSTANDING THE RELATIONSHIP BETWEEN GOD AND CHRIST

Many people erroneously teach and believe that Yeshu'a sits on the same pedestal as God. Yeshu'a Himself never taught that. The Bible does not teach that and early Christians did not believe it.

First Corinthians 15:27 says: "For he has put everything under his feet." When it says that "everything" has been put under him, it is clear that this does not include God Himself, who "put everything under Christ." From this we understand that it was God who "put everything under" Yeshu'a's feet.

To understand the relationship between God and Yeshu'a, it is helpful to understand the relationship between a head of state and a head of government.

The pharaoh who reigned in Egypt at the time Joseph lived there was the head of state of Egypt. Let us look into his relationship with Joseph.

Genesis 41:40 reads: "You shall be in charge of my palace, and all my people are to submit to your orders. Only with respect to the throne will I be greater than you." From this verse, we understand that while Pharaoh was the head of state, Joseph was the head of government.

In the sixteenth century, a doctrine in defense of monarchial absolutism, known as "divine right of kings" was established in Europe, which provides that a head of state be subject to no earthly authority because he or she derived his or her right to rule directly from God. Power resides in such heads of state, and they delegate it to whomsoever they will.

During the wars fought by Great Britain, the British prime minister (the head of government) led the war cabinet and coordinated the war effort. When the government defeated the enemy, it took the enemy's kingdom and put it under subjection to the then-reigning monarch on the throne of Great Britain (the head of state). As a specific example, when the British government sent a punitive expedition to the Benin Kingdom, after conquering it they made Ovoranmwen bow down to Queen Victoria's picture before exiling him.

God's head of government is Yeshu'a, and He is in charge of God's angelic army.

We see this confirmed in Mark 8:38: "If anyone is ashamed of me and my words in this adulterous and sinful generation, the Son of Man will be ashamed of them when he comes in his Father's glory with the holy angels."

We also see this precept in 1 Thessalonians 4:16: "For the Lord himself will come down from heaven, with a loud command, with the voice of the archangel and with the trumpet call of God, and the dead in Christ will rise first."

But when Yeshu'a has defeated the kingdom of Satan or Beelzebub, He Himself will be subject to God as 1 Corinthians 15: 28 informs us: "When he has done this, then the Son himself will be made subject to him who put everything under him, so that God may be all in all."

In fact, Yeshu'a is taking the kingdoms of this world in the name of God as verse 24 of that chapter teaches: "Then the end will come, when he hands over the kingdom to God the Father after he has destroyed all dominion, authority and power."

Thus far, it is established that Genesis 41:40 set the earthly precedent for the relationship between a head of state and a head of government. But let us look more closely at that word "government."

The word "government" originated from the Bible and not from ancient Greece or from philosophers. It appears twenty times in the Scriptures, and the very first time it was used as a noun directed to the future is in Isaiah 9:6: "For to us a child is born, to us a son is given, and the government will be on his shoulders. And he will be called Wonderful Counselor, Mighty God, Everlasting Father, Prince of Peace."

In Great Britain, the Queen is the head of state and she rules in her court. Now, there are certain protocols of court, which if breached, can lead to the Queen's disfavor. When Britain was an absolute monarchy, such a breach could cause one to be beheaded. So, to preserve the integrity and prestige of court, only a few people were allowed in court. These were aristocrats and well-bred people.

However, there was a challenge.

The Queen, as the ruler of Great Britain, had to rule over her people, but she could not grant all of them access to her throne. The solution was to create the office of prime minister to be a head of government that would be subject to the head of state and act as a mediator between the British people and their monarch. The people did not think of this idea themselves. It was an idea whose wisdom descended from heaven.

In fact, in 1066, when William of Normandy introduced the idea of a parliament, from which the prime minister emerged centuries later, members of William's Parliament were the lords (noblemen) and the ecclesiastics (clergy). This indicates that it was an idea whose origin was biblically inspired.

Now, let us consider again 1 Timothy 2:5: "For there is one God and one mediator between God and mankind, the man Christ Jesus." You see, Christ is the Mediator—the head of government.

Let us also take in 2 Corinthians 1:2-3: "Grace and peace to you from God our Father and the Lord Jesus Christ. Praise be to the God and Father of our Lord Jesus Christ, the Father of compassion and the God of all comfort."

Let us go deeper. Genesis 28:12 says: Jacob "had a dream in which he saw a stairway resting on the earth, with its top reaching to heaven, and the angels of God were ascending and descending on it." Here, we see that Jacob was dreaming. Now, you and I know that dreams recorded in the Bible are usually a picture of the future. So, ask yourself what was God trying to reveal to Jacob?

We know that angels are in the spiritual realm and man, as represented by Jacob, is in the physical realm. So, to bridge the gap between these two realms, we need what the NIV calls a "stairway" and the KJV calls a "ladder."

Let us consider John 1:51: "He then added, "Very truly I tell you, you will see 'heaven open, and the angels of God ascending and descending on' the Son of Man." Now, if you are not careful, you will think that the angels were descending and ascending in order to minister to Yeshu'a, but let us read that verse again. The NIV says they are ascending and descending "on" Yeshu'a. The KJV says they are ascending and descending "upon" Yeshu'a.

Notice that this verse and Genesis 28:12 are exactly the same, except that the word "ladder" and "stairway" have been replaced with the words "Son of Man."

What these verses are actually telling us when we make the spiritual connection between them is that Yeshu'a, who is the "Son of Man," is the ladder or stairway between the spiritual and the physical. Between God and man.

Why?

Because He is both Son of God and Son of Man.

Remember that Yeshu'a is the Second Adam. Now, look at what he calls Himself in John 1:51. He calls Himself the "Son of Man." Now look at what Adam is called in Luke 3:38: "… the son of Enosh, the son of Seth, the son of Adam, the son of God." Adam was never the Son of Man, but Yeshu'a is both Son of God and Son of Man.

There is a reason that Jacob had to be the man to catch that revelation. In Romans 1:16 we read: "I am not ashamed of the gospel, because it is the power of God that brings salvation to everyone who believes: first to the Jew, then to the Gentile."

Jacob was the human founder of the nation of Israel, and he, as the patriarch, saw that revelation because it is intended for the Jew first and then to us who are Gentiles (after the Jews have had the right of first refusal).

You see, the Jews are first and we are last.

This is the true meaning of Matthew 19:30: "But many who are first will be last, and many who are last will be first."

Now, we are separated from God when we sin. Habakkuk 1:13 helps us understand that God's purity is such that God cannot look on sin or have it come near Him. "You are of purer eyes than to behold evil, and cannot look on iniquity" (NKJV).

However, the Bible also shows us that God's love never ceases. This assurance is contained in Lamentations 3:22-23: "The steadfast love of the LORD never ceases; his mercies never come to an end; they are new every morning; great is your faithfulness" (ESV).

Now, let us consider Romans 8:38-39: "For I am convinced that neither death nor life, neither angels nor demons, neither the present nor the future, nor any powers, neither height nor depth, nor anything else in all creation, will be able to separate us from the love of God that is in Christ Jesus our Lord."

Finally, on this score, let us consider Isaiah 59:2: "But your iniquities have separated you from your God; your sins have hidden his face from you, so that he will not hear."

Notice that sin separates us from God, but it does not separate us from the love of God.

What is this love of God?

It is not a what, but a Who. Yeshu'a is the love of God.

That is why we need a mediator between God and man, because sin separates us from God. But here is what love does: 1 Peter 4:8 says, "Love covers over a multitude of sins."

Now, why are our sins forgiven or, in a sense, covered?

They are forgiven or covered because of the blood of Jesus. This is what John 3:16 has been saying for over two thousand years: "For God so loved the world, that he gave his only begotten Son, that whosoever believes in him should not perish, but have everlasting life."

Yeshu'a is the personification of the love of God.

THINK LIKE YESHU'A

What did Yeshu'a mean in Matthew 15:11 when he said, "Not that which goeth into the mouth defileth a man; but that which cometh out of the mouth, this defileth a man"?

Verse 18 of that same chapter gives insight into His meaning: "But those things which proceed out of the mouth come forth from the heart; and they defile the man."

To further understand what Yeshu'a means by "heart," we may consult His words in Matthew 9:4: "And Jesus knowing their thoughts said, Why think you evil in your hearts?"

From this verse, we understand that it is our words that defile us and poison our futures, but the words we speak are manufactured from our hearts and the process begins with our thoughts. So, to understand ourselves and others, we need to analyze thought processes. But the dilemma is, unlike Christ, none of us reads minds.

However, if we can spend enough time listening to people talk, over a period of time, we will find out that it is not possible for them to hide what is in their hearts. It must come out of their mouths, whether deliberately or inadvertently.

This is why psychiatrists ask us to lie down on a couch and talk.

Yeshu'a has already told us that our issues in life emanate from our thought life, which is expressed through our speech.

Now, that we know the problem, what is the solution?

Hebrews 12:2 gives us the solution: "Looking unto Jesus, the author and finisher of our faith." We resolve the issue of our thoughts and the words poisoning our lives by learning to think like Yeshu'a. If we study Yeshu'a's interactions with His disciples, we will see a positive relationship that instilled confidence and expanded the minds of illiterate men, to such an extent that they went on to change the world. How? By implementing the principles Yeshu'a taught them.

So, what was Yeshu'a's secret?

In the Gospels, we see that Yeshu'a empowered His disciples by connecting with them at least five times more than He corrected them.

He inspired them at least five times more than He disciplined them.

In the presence of Yeshu'a, the disciples felt they could do anything, which is why Peter walked on water at His command.

Most people erroneously think Yeshu'a interfered with the elements to allow Peter to walk on water. Not true. Peter walked on water because He believed in Yeshu'a, and the Scriptures confirm this.

Another word for belief is faith.

We see that when Yeshu'a went to His hometown, he could do no miracles because His kinsmen did not believe Him. Let us read Mark 6:5-6: "He could not do any miracles there, except lay his hands on a few sick people and heal them. He was amazed at their lack of faith." The reason Yeshu'a did not perform miracles in Nazareth is that the people there had no faith in God through Him.

One way we can train our minds to think like Yeshu'a is to train our mouths to talk like Him.

In our relationships with people, let us try to use Yeshu'a's 5-to-1 principle. We should have five times more positive conversations and encounters with people than negative ones.

Praise at least five times more than you criticize.

However, for this paradigm shift to be successful, and not perceived as flattery, we must link our positive words to the skills and efforts that drive the results we want to see in the people around us and in ourselves.

Have you experienced the dynamic where somebody is so greatly influenced by another person that if you want to change that first person's mind you say "go and fetch so and so, because he is the only one she listens to."

Conversely, have you noticed how we raise our guard around people who are negative and constantly criticize others?

The contrast in these two situations is because the influential person makes other people feel good by constantly affirming them. Subliminally, the person who is being affirmed identifies the person affirming them with positivity, and therefore will drop their guard when in the presence of that person. The reverse is the case with people who are overly critical

Do you know that ordinary human beings can have that type of relationship with God?

God has feelings. He, like us, likes to feel good. And if we can make God feel good about us, we will have much influence with Him.

God made us in order to receive pleasure from us. We see that in Revelations 4:11.

Hebrews 11:6 tells us "without faith it is impossible to please God." Yeshu'a understood this, which is why He said in Mark 11:22: "Have faith in God." Because He practiced that principle Himself, Yeshu'a pleased God and because He pleased God, God Himself said this about Yeshu'a: "This is my beloved Son, in whom I am well pleased" (Matthew 3:17).

Apply the 5-to-1 principle to prayer. Let your prayers consist of five times more thanksgiving to God than prayers that ask for things.

Look at Yeshu'a's prayers. He hardly ever asked for things. His prayers were typically "Thy Will be Done" prayers. And because of this, God gave Yeshu'a the things He did not even ask for.

This is the same principle used by Solomon. His prayer to God at Gibeon was centered around God's will, not His own. Solomon knew that Israel was special to God and that God wanted the nation of Israel to be an example to other nations. So when God asked Him for what he wanted, Solomon asked God to give him wisdom to lead Israel in the way that God wanted.

And because He did this, God gave Solomon things, which were far more than Solomon could have imagined.

Perhaps we do not have the things we want because we do not think about the things God wants. Yeshu'a and Solomon understood this principle found in Psalm 37:4: "Delight thyself also in the LORD; and he shall give thee the desires of thine heart."

Another thing we can learn from Yeshu'a's thought patterns, just by reading His words, is that He always thought the best about people. We see this in read John 8:10-11: "Jesus straightened up and asked her, 'Woman, where are they? Has no one condemned you?' 'No one, sir,' she said. 'Then neither do I condemn you,' Jesus declared. 'Go now and leave your life of sin.'"

This however does not mean He trusted people. John 2:24-25 gives us insight that He was careful with whom He confided. "But Jesus would not entrust himself to them, for he knew all people. He did not need any testimony about mankind, for he knew what was in each person."

Instead of assuming negative intentions, assume that people have positive intentions. That assumption creates a ripple effect that can overwhelm even people who do have bad intentions, causing them to refocus to good intentions. Even if it does not change their intentions to positive ones, it could frustrate their negative intention.

The reason this works is that it causes you and the belligerent person to move from the battleground to a common ground. You need an enemy to fight a war, and if the enemy refuses to play that role and chooses to be friendly, you cannot remain on the battleground alone.

Assuming good or bad intentions is just like a smile or a frown. You will notice that when you smile at people, they tend to smile back at you. But when you frown at people they also tend to frown back at you.

Perhaps the most important thing we learn from Yeshu'a's thinking is His concept of time.

On earth, we live in chronological time. This is the time sphere were you have the past, present and future. Now, because chronological time is interdependent, humans are vulnerable to regret about the past, anxiety in the present, and fear of the future.

The missing link in chronological time is knowledge. Hind sight, they say, is 20/20, so you know in full what you did in the past, but you cannot correct it. The present is shaped by the past, and so you have limited control over it. The future is unknown, so at best, all you can do is attempt to influence it.

However, the Bible makes us understand that the time zone in operation in God's Kingdom is simultaneous time. This means that concepts such as past, present, and future are not in operation. What exists is only in the now.

This is the reason Yeshu'a told the Pharisees in John 8:58 that "before Abraham was, I am." It is also the reason God, Yeshu'a, God's prophets, and angelic messengers of God often talk about the past, present and future as if they are one and the same. For instance, in Isaiah 46:10 God speaking through Isaiah says "I make known the end from the beginning, from ancient times, what is still to come."

This illustrates a basic difference between adults and children. Because they are fresh from God and still have their factory settings, children's concept of time is that everything happens now. They pray and immediately expect results. They enter the car and immediately expect to be at their destination.

You may say they are being childish, but is that not what Yeshu'a asked us to do in Mark 11:24: "Therefore I tell you, whatever you ask for in prayer, believe that you have received it, and it will be yours."

For example, man fell from grace in Genesis chapter 3, and Yeshu'a was born a man in order that He would redeem man back to grace, as is recorded in John 3:16. Between the time of the fall and the time of the redemption were at least four thousand years in chronological time. However, closer study of Scripture shows that the redemption was the subject of a specific prophecy in Genesis 3:15, four thousand years before it happened in chronological time.

But even these two events, from the point of view of Adam and Eve, were representative of the present and the future because they were living in chronological time.

However, when we read Revelations 13:8, Yeshu'a is referred to as "the Lamb slain from the foundation of the world." From this verse, we understand that the actual timing of Yeshu'a's sacrificial death for the redemption of mankind happened at the time when God laid the foundation of the world.

But how is this possible?

Because you and I live in chronological time or chronos, as it is known in the original Greek language, which means the sequential time of things happening after the other. But God lives in simultaneous time or simul in the original Latin, which means at the same time.

We also understand our conversion to the Christian faith by chronological time, and we say we were born again and baptized at such and such a time. But if we read Ephesians 1:4-5, we will see that God chose us before the foundation of this world was laid, before there was even any need to be born again.

Second Peter 3:8 and Psalm 90:4 are very instructive: "But do not forget this one thing, dear friends: With the Lord a day is like a thousand years, and a thousand years are like a day."

"A thousand years in your sight are like a day that has just gone by, or like a watch in the night."

These verses tell us that our concept of time is completely different from God's.

Now, why is it important to understand these concepts?

You and I are limited by chronos, but God and His Son are unlimited in simul. We know only the past and are knowing the present, while God and His Son know the past, present, and future at the same time.

Apostle Paul put it best when he said in 1 Corinthians 13:9-10 that "we know in part and we prophesy in part, but when completeness comes, what is in part disappears."

Completeness comes when we transition from chronos to simul time.

However, before that "completeness" comes, we who live in chronos and trust in God and His Son, Yeshu'a, can trust and believe when they tell us through the mouth of Paul, "do not be anxious about anything, but in every situation, by prayer and petition, with thanksgiving, present your requests to God."

Pretend you are in a submarine and you suspect that you are heading for a rock that will sink the submarine and kill you and your fellow sailors. You would naturally be anxious.

But if your superior officer looks through the periscope and sees your destination, rather than rocks, and tells you what he has seen, you would have no need to be anxious. You then understand that while you only know where you are coming from and where you are, your superior officer knows where you are coming from, where you are, as well as where you are headed.

In the same vein, the reason our attitudes should be that of hopefulness, which must be expressed in our thinking, behavior, facial expressions, and our manner of speech, is because our Creator and His Only Begotten Son, who can see our past, present and future, has told us not to be anxious about tomorrow. Having therefore this type of assurance, what is the need for worry?

To perfect our mind-transformation process, we need to begin to think like Yeshu'a in terms of simultaneous time rather than chronological time.

If we want to spark creativity and possibilities in others and in ourselves, we have to inspire people to shift their consciousness from chronos time to simul time by not belaboring them with deadlines, timeframes, and other units of tying productivity to time. That belaboring focuses their attention on chronos time, and the more attention they pay to the passage of time, the more pressure they are under. The more pressure they are under, the less likely they are to be productive.

Why? Because chronos time is constantly diminishing, but simul time is constantly replenishing. You experience fatigue in chronological time and you experience refreshing from simultaneous time. This is biblical.

Let us read Acts 3:19. It says: "Repent ye therefore, and be converted, that your sins may be blotted out, when the times of refreshing shall come from the presence of the Lord."

What made man fall from grace? The answer is sin. What happened when Adam and Eve were kicked out of paradise? They began to live by the sweat of their brows. This is recorded in Genesis 3:17. Notice that it was the ground that was cursed to man in Genesis 3:17, not man himself. What we read in Acts 3:19 above is the effect of the undoing of the curse of Genesis 3:17.

Finally, the story of Yeshu'a and the invalid at the pool of Bethesda is a classic example of the paradigm difference between chronos time and simul time. When Yeshu'a met the invalid, the man was waiting for the time when the angel would trouble the water. This is why when Yeshu'a asked him if he wanted to get well, the invalid started to talk about his limitations (see John 5:7.)

The reason for this behavior is that the chronological sequence of time will focus you on your limitations. The invalid was clearly focused on chronos time, because if you read John 5:4 in the NIV it begins with the words "from time to time." God is telling us that many of our problems spring from our focus on chronos.

That is why Yeshu'a, in Mark 11:24, said when we pray to God we should act as if He has already given what we asked for, because He exists in simultaneous time and by virtue of James 1:17, every good gift comes from that sphere.

So, remember, you and I may not have access to everything the future holds, but God and His Son do. One of the purposes of life, therefore, is to find out whether we will trust God. When we live in anxiety and worry about the future, we are exhibiting symptoms of the fact that we do not trust God. When this happens to us, it helps to consider that although we currently exist in chronos time, God and His Son, exist in simul time. This knowledge has the effect of refocusing our minds from our present circumstances to the promise of Romans 8:28, which promises that God is working all things for the good of those who love Him. I believe that as you make this practice a habit, it will have the same effect on you that it has had on me—peace.

THE FAVORITE CHILD

Sometimes, when I preach the John 3:16 message, people ask me how I know God loves them. If they are parents, I ask them if any of their children looks like them, and then I ask why they love that child. It is a natural tendency to love a child that looks like you. I am guilty of that myself. This is at the core of why God loves us. Genesis 1:26 says, "God said, Let us make man in our image, after our likeness: and let them have dominion." Verse 27 goes further to say, "So God created man in his own image, in the image of God created he him." God loves you and me because we are created in His image.

When you understand this fundamental principle, you will stop trying to earn God's love and just accept it. God loves us because of what we are—His image. David understood this principle, and in my opinion, that understanding was a major factor in God's pronouncement of David as a man after His heart. David was very conscious of being created in God's image.

Many people who believe in the divine will wake up and proceed to either pray or read their sacred Scripture. After that, the next thing most people would do (and I have asked around) is look in the mirror.

David did that. But instead of seeing himself in the mirror, guess what David saw?

Psalm 17:15 tells us: As for me, I will be vindicated and will see your face; when I awake, I will be satisfied with seeing your likeness (NIV).

When David looked in the mirror, he did not see himself. He saw God in him. This made him love himself more because he loved God and God was in him. Moreover, because he loved himself, he was able to love others.

Consider what Yeshu'a told us in the greatest commandment: "'Love the Lord your God with all your heart and with all your soul and with all your mind.' This is the first and greatest commandment. And the second is like it: 'Love your neighbor as yourself'"" (Matthew 22-37-38 NIV).

The continuum of growth in love as shown by Yeshu'a is that we must first love God, then proceed to love ourselves, and have that same love for our neighbors. You cannot love others unless you love yourself. And you cannot love yourself unless you love God.

In essence, we are God's favorite creation—His favorite children. God created us to have "dominion." However, many humans and even believers do not have dominion.

I have thought and prayed about this situation of not having dominion, and after meditating on Bible verses, putting their instructions to practice, and seeing them work for me, I have come to realize that we do not have dominion because we are too far removed from God.

Even in the natural, the more a prince draws closer to his father, the King, the more authority he wields. The more you and I draw nearer to God, who gave us dominion, the more dominion we will wield.

Now, the Enemy may want to corrupt our acceptance of the dominion freely given to us by God by making us think that man has lost his God-given dominion. Satan may be the prince of this world, but even now and all the times before, people who know where they stand in God have always had dominion.

In Genesis 1:28, we read "God said unto them, Be fruitful, and multiply, and replenish the earth, and subdue it: and have dominion" (KJV).

In understanding our powers to dominate the earth, it is necessary to read Psalm 8:6: "You made them rulers over the works of your hands; you put everything under their feet." This verse shows that David was conversant with Genesis 1:28 and knew that God never reversed Genesis 1:28.

A child should be like the parent. Remember the saying, like father like son?

Who is your father?

In Genesis 1:2-3, God saw darkness and did not describe what He saw with His words. He changed what He saw with His words. God saw darkness and said, "Let there be light!"

In Joel 3:10 we read: "Let the weak say, I am strong" (KJV).

God sees a weakling and says to him, you are strong.

As a child of God, always remember that the primary purpose for which God created words was as tools of creation. Communication is a secondary purpose of words. Your words are not meant to describe your situation, they are meant to create your situation.

Consider the Nobel Prize. Have you noticed that they give Nobel prizes to novelists, writers, and poets, but they do not give Nobel prizes to journalists? Journalists get a Pulitzer Prize, which is a very high award, but nowhere near the Nobel Prize. The reason is that journalists report what they see while novelists, writers, and poets create characters and places that previously did not exist. The journalist is a reporter but the novelists, writers, and poets are creators. People who create are more relevant than people who report.

Now, we are God's favorite children. The knowledge of that should lead us to the further knowledge that other people are also His favorite children. Because of this, be careful how you treat people, especially those under your influence.

How do you treat your wife, your children, and your subordinates?

David said in Psalm 6:1: "LORD, do not rebuke me in your anger or discipline me in your wrath." David here is teaching us a very important principle that is necessary for every parent or person in authority. Do not correct children or subordinates when you are angry or full of wrath. Build up yourself to the point where your first instinct is to show love publicly and to defend your wife, your children, and your subordinates. And if you must discipline them, do so behind closed doors.

This builds a bond between you and your wife, your children, and your subordinates.

In Matthew 12:1 and 2, the Pharisees accused Yeshu'a's disciples because they ate corn from the fields on the Sabbath. If you read the verses immediately after, you will see how Yeshu'a instinctively and automatically defended His subordinates against the accusation of the Pharisees saying, "Haven't you read what David did when he and his companions were hungry? He entered the house of God, and he and his companions ate the consecrated bread—which was not lawful for them to do, but only for the priests. Or haven't you read in the Law that the priests on Sabbath duty in the temple desecrate the Sabbath and yet are innocent?" (Matt. 12:3-5 NIV).

That Yeshu'a defended them so vehemently strengthened the bond He had with His disciples and made them more committed to Him.

Since we are favorite children of the kingdom, we ought to walk according to how the kingdom walks, not how the world walks, because we are not of the world. Second Corinthians 5:7 teaches us that we walk by faith not by sight.

I want to give a literal example of that verse.

Matthew 14:28-31 gives an account of how Peter was able to walk on water. It reads: "Lord, if it's you," Peter replied, "tell me to come to you on the water." "Come," he said. Then Peter got down out of the boat, walked on the water, and came toward Jesus. However, when he saw the wind, he was afraid and, beginning to sink, cried out, "Lord, save me!" Immediately Jesus reached out his hand and caught him. "You of little faith," he said, "why did you doubt?"(NIV).

Notice that it was faith in Yeshu'a that gave Peter the confidence to walk on water, but immediately when he "saw," he began to drown.

Why? Because we are to walk by faith not by sight!

Sometimes you just feel led to do something, and you start to do it, then your carnal mind starts to feed you with logic and you begin to see. Then your faith disappears and you begin to fall. Nothing cancels out faith like logic, and the children of this world are so full of logic that they can reason you out of your faith.

What is the Word of God? John 1:1 teaches us that Yeshu'a is the Word of God. Romans 10:17 teaches us that faith comes by hearing the Word of God.

Thus, as long as Peter's attention was focused on Yeshu'a, who is the Word of God, he had faith. But when his attention turned to the boisterous winds, which represents the world, the faith disappeared.

This is what happens to most of us. How much time do we spend focused on the Word of God? How much time do you spend focused on God?

David gave a timeless warning in Psalm 10:4: "In his pride the wicked man does not seek him; in all his thoughts there is no room for God."

Is there room in your thoughts for God? How often do you think of your problems? How often do you think of God? If you tabulate the data, to which do we give more attention, God or our challenges?

The answer to that question determines whether we are walking on water or sinking.

I was at a luxury retail outlet and their clothes and accessories were generally nice, but one of them was mega expensive. I asked why. and was told it was costly because it was handmade.

It got me thinking about the creation process in Genesis chapter 1. Do you know that God spoke into existence everything that was created on earth, but only of man was it said, "God formed a man" (Genesis 2:7). You and I are hand made by God, and that is the reason we have the highest value to Him of all created things.

So be careful that you do not waste your hand-made body, soul, and spirit in pursuit of material things that were spoken into existence. "For what shall it profit a man, if he shall gain the whole world, and lose his own soul?" (Mark 8:36).

FROM ZERO TO HERO

Many times, Satan uses a trick to deceive us about our true spiritual state. I call it the water trick. Satan wants us to have a false sense of security by believing that we are not as sinful as other people are. His desire is that we will look down on others because, in our estimation, we are more righteous than they are.

Consider the fallacy in this tactic. Isn't it impossible to have water that is "a little" dirty? Can you imagine a cup of water containing just a little bacteria laughing at a bucket of muddy water because it is undrinkable? No! They are both undrinkable!

Humans are like water and our sins have made us impure. The bottom line is that we are all undrinkable!

As the Scripture says: "For all have sinned and fall short of the glory of God" (Romans 3:23). It doesn't matter how short you came if you did not make the grade. So do not look down on others. When you do, you are falling for Satan's water trick.

Sometimes, the muddiest water is better than the deceptive sample that looks pure, but is not tasted for the simple reason that its need for purification is apparent. The other can stay a lifetime without anyone knowing that it is impure!

None of us is made righteous by our acts. As 2 Corinthians 5:21 teaches, "God made him who had no sin to be sin for us, so that in him we might become the righteousness of God." And just as we observed in the previous chapter, we must remember this message especially when dealing with our children or with people over whom we have some authority, like our subordinates at work.

Everybody wants affirmation. The biggest mistake we can make is to think that only children want attention. An eighty-year-old man can be playing golf, and if he makes a hole in one, he wants people to see him.

Unfortunately, most people focus attention on others, especially on those they have influence, only when they misbehave. When this happens, subliminally, the person starts to relate misbehavior with attention. Since God hard-wired us to crave attention, and if the only way to get it is by misbehaving, many people will develop a habit of misbehaving which becomes a life style, then a destiny.

Do you want people around you to exhibit good behavior? Catch them doing something good and focus attention on them at that instant.

God gave Yeshu'a a great deal of attention, even to the extent that He said, "This is My beloved Son, in whom I am well pleased" (Matthew 3:17). Because of this positive attention, we read in Acts 10:38 that Yeshu'a "went about doing good."

The problem that makes a lot of us focus our attention on correcting negative behavior instead of rewarding good behavior is that we compare ourselves and those close to us with others. Too many children of God have been so caught up in the cares of this world, otherwise called the artificial reality created by the Enemy, that we whom the Scriptures call a "peculiar people" are alarmed when we do not fit in in the world and among worldly people. We want to be considered normal and usual. We want to belong.

Man's natural habitat, the one God designed for him, is a paradise called Eden; this world is an insane asylum under a ruler called Satan. If you "fit in" in Satan's world, and there is no difference between you and the children of his world, then you must consider whether you are truly in the faith.

Do you think Yeshu'a was considered normal while He was on the earth? Let us consider an encounter he had with His family. "When his family heard about this, they went to take charge of him, for they said, "He is out of his mind" (Mark 3:21).

When Moses was born, his parents "saw that God had given them an unusual child, and they were not afraid to disobey the king's command" (Hebrews 11:23).

So do not be alarmed when you stand out and are said to be unusual in this world. It ought to be so. You are described as "a chosen generation, a royal priesthood, an holy nation, a peculiar people" (1 Peter 2:9).

Many people go through life with unnecessarily low self-esteem because they see themselves from the prism of their history and ancestry rather than how God sees them. God sees us as heroes, but because some of us come from homes that are not considered wealthy or accomplished (according to the standards set by this present world system administered by Satan), we see ourselves as zeroes. This disconnects many from their God-given potential.

This was the case with Gideon. "Lord," Gideon replied, "how can I rescue Israel? My clan is the weakest in the whole tribe of Manasseh, and I am the least in my entire family!" (Judges 6:15). But this is how God saw Gideon: "The angel of the LORD appeared to him and said, "Mighty hero, the LORD is with you!" (Judges 6:12). It was clear that Gideon's self-esteem issues came from his ties to his ancestry. Do not tie yourself to your history or ancestry. Tie yourself to God's vision of you! God sees you as a hero; do not see yourself as a zero.

Some of us feel unworthy because our parents told us we will never amount to much. Alternatively, it may have been a pastor or a prophet or our boss, or perhaps somebody we look up to, who sent us that negative message.

God does want us to honor our parents. We came through our father and our mother. However, we did not come from them. Even if our parents habitually make us feel unworthy, or if we still feel unloved, we owe a duty to God to honor them in spite of that.

Now I want to take the opportunity to teach on the real meaning of the word "father," so we can put it in proper perspective and relate it to ourselves.

God told us through Yeshu'a in Matthew 23:9: "Do not call anyone on earth 'father,' for you have one Father, and he is in heaven." This Scripture is not ambiguous. Apart from your biological father, no one on earth is deserving of the title Father or other acronyms for father such as daddy, papa, or what have you. This is why the Lord's Prayer begins with "Our Father" (Matthew 6:9). Respect men of God. Honor them. But do not violate God's commands to please pastors or other men of God or raise them to the status of Father. No matter how large their congregation or anointing may be, the highest any one should ask of you is "follow my example, as I follow the example of Christ" (1 Corinthians 11:1). Do not alter Scripture to fit your church, rather, alter your church to fit Scripture.

So if even our biological father or anybody who stands in authority over us habitually puts us down, we need to get a proper understanding that God is our Father. See yourself as He sees you. In Psalm 27:10 we read: "When my father and my mother forsake me, then the LORD will take me up."

Some of us have been Christians from our childhood and sometimes, particularly if we came to Christ through a strict, religious, and enemy-focused ministry, we tend to have a persecution mentality because people reviled us, stigmatized us, or generally persecuted us when we were growing up. If you grew up with that type of orientation, there are two things you need to be aware of:

The first is that you should not allow anybody to sell you the idea that a Christian is meant to be a boring, dour, and colorless human being. Yeshu'a was not like that. On earth, He was a fun person to be around, a sociable person who attended get-togethers and visited people (see Matthew 9:10, Luke 14:1, Luke 19:5). He was also very affectionate (John 13:23-25), yet He had authority and commanded respect (Matthew 7:29). Jesus dressed well (John 19:23), wore perfumes (Mark 14:3-6) and used to sing hymns with His disciples (Matthew 26:30). Now if Hebrews 12:2 admonishes us to "fix our eyes on Jesus, the author and perfecter of our faith," how then can you follow Jesus without exhibiting His qualities?

The second is that if you know Scripture, you should not be offended, upset, or downcast when you face insults, persecutions, stigmatization, and the like because of your faith. We see this precept in Matthew 5:11: "Blessed are you when people insult you, persecute you and falsely say all kinds of evil against you because of me."

So do not hold grudges against people who caused you pain and sabotaged your sense of self-esteem when you were growing up.

Have you ever signaled in traffic because you wanted to enter a lane, but the person behind would not let you in. So you go farther along in front and another driver lets you in, thereby putting you ahead of the driver who would not let you in? That is a case of traffic imitating life.

Do not hold grudges against people who blocked your progress earlier on in life. If they had not stopped your progress, somebody in your future would not have given you the chance that put you ahead of them. Just as Joseph said to his brothers, "As for you, ye thought evil against me; but God meant it unto good, to bring to pass, as it is this day, to save much people alive" (Genesis 50:20).We all have had such experiences in our lives. Unfortunately, rather than respond like Joseph did, we hold grudges against such people.

As I close this chapter, I think it is necessary to state that a pastor should not be just a motivational speaker, like Dr. Phil or Oprah. It is good to make people feel good, but the only lasting way that people can feel good is for them to be good. And for them to be good they have to confront their besetting sins and overcome them.

The New Testament contains the four Gospels, Acts, and other books as well. The Gospels are the good news that Yeshu'a died for our salvation. However, the other portions of the New Testament serve as a mirror for us. The whole purpose of a mirror is to see the imperfections in our appearance so we can make adjustments. When we remove the mirror (ignore the rest of the New Testament) and make Christianity about feeling good without being good, we sacrifice character building for momentary excitement. The problem is, when the storms of life come, we survive by character formed from the Word, not excitement. This type of "exciting" Christianity makes us think that God was created for us instead of the reality that we were created for God. "Therefore everyone who hears these words of Mine and acts on them, may be compared to a wise man who built his house on the rock. And the rain fell, and the floods came, and the winds blew and slammed against that house; and yet it did not fall, for it had been founded on the rock" (Matthew 7:24-25).

God has revealed two aspects of His personality to us. First John 4:8: "Whoever does not love does not know God, because God is love," teaches us that God Himself is love. Likewise, we are told in Isaiah 11:2: "The Spirit of the LORD will rest on him—the Spirit of wisdom and of understanding," that His Spirit is a spirit of wisdom. Thus, to be a successful Christ-follower, we need to foster both love and wisdom.

The love that God is is not an emotional love. It is an all-encompassing love whose qualities are expressed in detail in Galatians 5:22: "The fruit of the Spirit is love, joy, peace, forbearance, kindness, goodness, faithfulness."

Love makes us attractive to people, and we are most like God when we love. However, for unconditional love (what we know as agape love), to be effective, it must not be blind. You can love people unconditionally, but you do not love them blindly. You love them wisely.

If all we have as Christians is love, we may become vulnerable to ruthless people, and we will find that we are unable to control our passions. God did not give us passions so that they can control us. No. Passions are meant to fuel us and inspire us do difficult things as though they were easy.

That is one end of the love-wisdom scale.

If we have wisdom without love, we will end up becoming wily and skilled manipulators. The patriarch Jacob comes to mind here. He was blessed by God, but he was also wily, crafty, and not above pulling a smart one on people. He used his knowledge of God's principles to his advantage and this caused bitterness and resentment both with his brother, Esau, and with his uncle Laban.

Basically, all God wants from us is that we radiate love— the type of love described in 1 Corinthians 13:1-5: "Love is patient, love is kind. It does not envy, it does not boast, it is not proud. It does not dishonor others, it is not self-seeking, it is not easily angered, it keeps no record of wrongs."

The reason God wants us to have this singular nature is because man's natural habitat is a paradise. The Garden of Eden was God's extension of His Kingdom to earth. In God's Kingdom, all you need is love. You do not need wisdom. Why? In Ecclesiastes 7:12 we are told that "wisdom is a defense."

Look at the words "wisdom is a defense." We only need a defense when we are going to be attacked. If we are never going to be attacked, then we do not need a defense, right?

In Isaiah 2:4, the prophet prophesies that we will have no need of arms in God's Kingdom. In God's Kingdom we are never going to be attacked, which is why we do not need wisdom there. All we need us love.

So why do we need wisdom now?

If you know any loving, sweet, innocent, and pure people, you will notice that they are very easy to deceive. Adam and Eve were such people—full of love, but devoid of wisdom, even though they had intelligence, which tells us that intelligence is not wisdom.

If they had had wisdom, it is unlikely that the serpent would have been able to deceive them. But because of their simplicity, which was a function of their innocence, which was a function of their extremely loving and pure nature, they were deceived. In addition, in Genesis 3 it says that Eve wanted the wisdom that the tree offered. She apparently knew she did not have it but was deceived to believe she needed it.

Now let us see the warning Paul gave to us in 2 Corinthians 11:3: "But I fear, lest by any means, as the serpent beguiled Eve through his subtlety, so your minds should be corrupted from the simplicity that is in Christ." From this verse, we learn that it was the simplicity and the purity of Adam and Eve that made them vulnerable.

Does this mean we should become complicated and impure? God forbid. What it means is that we have to add wisdom to our simplicity and purity because we have an enemy that attacks us. And as we have already learned from Ecclesiastes 7:12, wisdom is a defense!

Agape love should lead us to extend smart love and not have blind love. Most of the problems Christ-followers have on earth are because they have no balance between love and wisdom.

One thing you will notice about sweet, loving people is that they tend to be gentle. Yet look at what the Bible says in Matthew 10:16: "Behold, I send you forth as sheep in the midst of wolves: be ye therefore wise as serpents, and harmless as doves." (KJV) Therefore, the type of Christianity where we are just full of love and trust and believe everything we are told by everyone is not a Christianity that honors Christ.

Christ identifies two things about His followers:

The first is in John 13:35, "By this everyone will know that you are my disciples, if you love one another."

The second is from Luke 21:15: "I will give you words and wisdom that none of your adversaries will be able to resist or contradict."

God does not want us to be cynical and distrustful of everyone, always praying enemy-focused prayers because we are so wise that we cannot relax. God wants us to have a balance.

Let us consider some examples of these two extremes.

In Judges 16:4-10 we read how Samson loved Delilah, yet every time he revealed his secrets to her, she would sell him out to his enemies. After the first time she deceived him, one would expect that he would learn. Yet, time after time, he continued to extend blind love to her instead of smart love, and in the end, she destroyed him. This is love without wisdom.

In Samuel 16:20-23 and 2 Samuel 17:23 we are introduced to Ahitiphel. He had wisdom, but no love. He stabbed his benefactor, David, in the back (figuratively), and in the end, he committed suicide because his wisdom could not compensate for his lack of love!

Now, let us consider an example of balance between love and wisdom.

In John 2:23-25, we see that Yeshu'a loved His disciples. He defended and protected them, yet He did not make Himself vulnerable to them, because He knew the limitations of men.

With many of us, a person may say to us "I love you," and they really mean it because they are being led by their emotions while in that sensual state where they must proclaim their undying devotion. We reciprocate by exposing ourselves emotionally and revealing our vulnerabilities. Eventually, when that soulful, emotional love clears, it is precisely what we told them in our time of passion that they use against us—just like Delilah did to Samson. This can be done to us by both male and female.

First, John 4:8 says God is love.

Proverbs 3:19 says by wisdom God created this earth.

In essence, who God is, is love. What God does is wisdom.

Satan (as Lucifer) was one of the most intelligent angels God created, but because he did not have righteous character, God demoted him. In making decisions to promote, God looks to a person's character, where men may look to their intelligence.

Think about this for a moment. How much of our intelligence can we ascribe to ourselves? Whether we have a sharp mind and are able to analyze issues or dissect them clinically, those abilities are gifts from God. But virtues like faithfulness, patience, long-suffering, and tolerance are things that we have to develop with discipline. Yeshu'a was the most intelligent man who ever walked the earth, but listen to the reason God gave for promoting Him: "Being found in appearance as a man, he humbled himself by becoming obedient to death—even death on a cross! Therefore God exalted him to the highest place and gave him the name that is above every name" (Philippians 2:8). Yeshu'a's promotion by God was a function of His character, not His intelligence. You and I will be promoted to the degree of the improvement in our character.

Now, let us gain some insight into how a person who is balanced in love and wisdom thinks of him or herself.

If we do not love ourselves, we will constantly keep changing our God-given personality to please others. This can go on for a lifetime. But it does not have to be so. Take some time to fall in love with yourself. So what if others say you are too "into" yourself? If we do not love ourselves, how can we obey God's commandment to us to love others as we love ourselves? If we hate ourselves, we cannot obey that commandment.

Wisdom lets us understand that it is better to like ourselves and let others dislike us in the process than to dislike ourselves to make others like us. Matthew 22:39 says: "Love your neighbor as yourself," not love your neighbor better than yourself!

Why is it important to know this?

Remember that in God's kingdom, all you need is love. But while we are on earth, we need wisdom because we have an Enemy that hates us and wants to steal our goods, kill us, and destroy our purpose. Only wisdom can make us understand why Satan hates us and empower us to overcome him.

In conclusion, let us again ponder why Jesus wept.

The reason Jesus wept at Lazarus' tomb is the same reason Satan smiles: doubt. Faith please God and displeases Satan, while doubt displeases God and pleases Satan. But you cannot understand faith and apply it properly if you do not understand love. They are inextricably connected, both in this world and in the world to come, so much so that 1 Corinthians 13:13 says: "And now these three remain: faith, hope and love. But the greatest of these is love."

Hebrews 11:6 tell us that "without faith, it is impossible to please God." However, without love, it is impossible to have the faith that pleases God. What then is faith? How can we define it?

I believe that faith is the product of love and wisdom. Essentially, faith is right belief. In 1 Corinthians 13:7 we are taught that love "believes all things" (KJV). In Ecclesiastes 10:10, King Solomon taught that "wisdom is profitable to direct" (KJV). Faith, therefore, is the ability to believe all things that are true as directed by God's Spirit of Wisdom, which leads us into all truth. This is corroborated by John 16:13: "But when he, the Spirit of truth, comes, he will guide you into all the truth."

The Spirit is not guiding us into all truth so we can just be informed. No. Every item of information that does not lead to transformation is simply entertainment. He is guiding us into His truths so we can believe them, and it is that faith, that product of love and wisdom, which pleases God and His Son, Jesus. It was for lack of it that Jesus wept.

As you read this and the Spirit ministers to you, I pray you will grow in the type of faith that pleases God and His Son, the type of faith that moves mountains, and the type of faith that allows other "Kingdom keys" to be released to the believer. These keys include: sowing and reaping, friendship with God, avoiding criticism, managing yourself and your relationships, growing in the Spirit, renewing your mind, harnessing the creative power of words, loving your enemies, understanding the relationship between God and Jesus, thinking like Yeshu'a, understanding that you are the favorite child, and moving from zero to hero.

My prayer is that we will all attain to this type of faith in Jesus' name, and that where Jesus once wept because of the lack of it, He will smile on us as we exhibit it and teach others to do the same. Amen.

www.ingramcontent.com/pod-product-compliance
Lightning Source LLC
LaVergne TN
LVHW051132080426
835510LV00018B/2378